"Every generation has the responsibility to pass on the evangelical heritage of the Reformation to the next generation. At the core of this heritage is the gospel of salvation by grace alone through faith alone in Christ alone. However, no less central to the Reformation are the divine authority of Scripture alone and worship to the glory of God alone. Even in this day of resurgent Calvinism, many Christians might be surprised to learn that Calvin placed worship according to God's commandment alongside the gospel as the two chief doctrines by which Christianity maintains its vital force—the very soul that animates the church. At a time when many evangelical Christians relegate the methods of the church to the pragmatism of 'whatever works,' Calvin's treatise is a silver trumpet sounding a clarion call to return to simple obedience to God's Word."

—DR. JOEL R. BEEKE
President and professor of systematic
theology and homiletics
Puritan Reformed Theological Seminary
Grand Rapids, Mich.

"Among Calvin's many treatises and letters, these two are outstanding and deserve your close attention. They were written at a turning period in his ministry and at a crucial point in the history of the Reformation. They reveal his gifts as a humanist scholar, as a defender of the Reformation, and as a pastor who cared for the spiritual well-being of the flock. He knew that the Reformation had recovered the gospel and that Rome sought to persuade evangelicals to sell their birthright for a pottage of salvation by grace and works. These are truths we need to hear and learn again."

—DR. R. SCOTT CLARK
Professor of church history and historical theology
Westminster Seminary California
Escondido, Calif.

"For those who wrestle with the place of the church in the midst of change and challenges, this new translation of *The Necessity of Reforming the Church* will be a welcome guide. Though it was written in a time so different from ours, its pastoral and practical teachings on the Word of God and the church remain relevant as it offers clarity and priority, qualities we often lack in the present-day church."

—REV. JOEL E. KIM
President
Westminster Seminary California
Escondido, Calif.

"I am delighted that these tracts by Calvin are now available in convenient form and fresh translation. Both his *A Reply to Sadoleto* and *The Necessity of Reforming the Church* direct us to the heart of Calvin's pursuit of reformation: the worship, doctrine, discipline, and sacraments of the church. Here we do not find the eloquent prose of the *Institutes*, honed through several decades in five editions, but the passionate rhetoric that is reminiscent of Luther's 1520 tracts. Calvin's question must be pondered by today's officers of Christ's church: 'since God . . . openly hates what we support for worshiping Him beyond His command, what do we profit by doing anything to the contrary?' Now as then, the 'infinite forest' of corruptions in worship and polity entails 'monstrosities of idolatry' and exercises 'harsh and especially harmful tyranny over souls.' This is essential reading for understanding Calvin's faithfulness in serving Christ's church."

—JOHN R. MUETHER
Dean of libraries and professor of church history
Reformed Theological Seminary
Orlando, Fla.

"Written in the mid-sixteenth century, these two works by John Calvin are as relevant today as they were in those days. The twenty-first century church must hear Calvin's arguments about the need for reformation according to the Word of God. Unfortunately, many churches in the Protestant tradition have fallen back into the theological deviations and errors of the Roman Catholic Church during the medieval period. Not a few have swerved from the simplicity of worship that God revealed in the Scriptures and introduced other gospels, such as the theology of prosperity, the movement of signs and wonders, and the modern apostolic movement with its Judaizing teaching. On the other hand, churches that were once Reformed have adopted theological liberalism and let themselves be seduced by modern culture, accepting immoral behaviors clearly condemned in the Scriptures. Let us heed Calvin's call for a reformation in our day."

—Dr. Augustus Nicodemus Lopes
Vice president of the Presbyterian Church of Brazil
Assistant pastor of First Presbyterian Church
of Recife, Brazil

"What a great treasure Reformation Trust has opened to us with this wonderful new translation by Casey Carmichael of two of Calvin's most important works. Here speaks the well-trained lawyer pleading for the case of Christ's church in his impressive letter to Sadoleto and his formidable exposition on what the church of Christ needs to be alive and dynamic. These words were written down long ago, but every reader will see that they are as relevant for today's church as never before. Calvin wanted to serve God and His people, and he still does, as this work shows. So, let's start using this rich, scriptural material for the well-being of the church and for the glory of God."

—Dr. Herman Selderhuis
President, Theological University Apeldoorn
Director, Refo500

The Necessity of Reforming the Church

Foreword by W. Robert Godfrey

The
NECESSITY
of
REFORMING
the
CHURCH

with A Reply to Cardinal Sadoleto

JOHN CALVIN | *Translated by Casey Carmichael*

ℝ *Reformation Trust*   A DIVISION OF LIGONIER MINISTRIES, ORLANDO, FL

The Necessity of Reforming the Church
© 2020 by Ligonier Ministries
© 2020 Foreword by W. Robert Godfrey

Published by Reformation Trust Publishing
a division of Ligonier Ministries
421 Ligonier Court, Sanford, FL 32771
Ligonier.org   ReformationTrust.com

Printed in Crawfordsville, Indiana
LSC Communications
00001020

ISBN 978-1-64289-287-1 (Hardcover)
ISBN 978-1-64289-288-8 (ePub)
ISBN 978-1-64289-289-5 (Kindle)

Cover design: Ligonier Creative
Interior design and typeset: Katherine Lloyd, The DESK

Scripture quotations in the foreword are from the ESV® Bible (The Holy Bible, English Standard Version®), copyright © 2001 by Crossway, a publishing ministry of Good News Publishers. Used by permission. All rights reserved.

Library of Congress Cataloging-in-Publication Data

Names: Calvin, Jean, 1509-1564, author. | Carmichael, Casey, translator.
Title: The necessity of reforming the church / by John Calvin ; translated by Casey Carmichael ; foreword by W. Robert Godfrey.
Description: Orlando, FL : Reformation Trust Publishing, a division of Ligonier Ministries, 2020. | Includes index.
Identifiers: LCCN 2020010353 (print) | LCCN 2020010354 (ebook) | ISBN 9781642892871 (hardcover) | ISBN 9781642892888 (epub) | ISBN 9781642892895 (kindle edition)
Subjects: LCSH: Reformation. | Church reform. | Church--Authority. | Calvin, Jean, 1509-1564--Correspondence. | Sadoleto, Jacopo, 1477-1547.
Classification: LCC BR301 .C2813 2020 (print) | LCC BR301 (ebook) | DDC 262.001/7--dc23
LC record available at https://lccn.loc.gov/2020010353
LC ebook record available at https://lccn.loc.gov/2020010354

CONTENTS

FOREWORD

W. Robert Godfrey

Jesus Christ said, "I will build my church, and the gates of hell shall not prevail against it," establishing the church as the very center of His redeeming work. Jesus is gathering a people. Jesus is creating a new humanity, and that is the church. Yet, when you look at the history of the church, you very soon discover that the church needs to be reformed over and over again. The church declines in its theology or life and then needs to be reordered, renewed, revived, restructured, and reshaped according to its problems. According to Christ's promise, the church does not fail entirely, but it can run seriously astray.

The repeated need for reform is not because Christ's work to save His people was not finished and perfect, nor because God's Word is not clear in directing the church, but because the church is composed of sinners. Even sinners saved by grace not only get things wrong morally, but they get things wrong intellectually and theologically and liturgically and ecclesiastically. Here is the reason why the church is constantly going off track.

We see that in the Old Testament. The psalmist writes in Psalm 80: "Restore us, O God; let your face shine, that we may be saved! O Lord God of hosts, how long will you be angry with your people's prayers?" (vv. 3–4). The people in the old covenant experienced that alienation from God from time to time and had to pray that they might be restored. We see it also in the New Testament. Paul had to write to the Corinthian church to reform it and correct its serious problems. We might be surprised that a church founded by an Apostle could so quickly get so much wrong. Yet that is exactly what we find. The truth that the church needs to be reformed from time to time is clearly taught in the Bible.

The great Reformation of the sixteenth century was one of the most needed and fundamental reforms of the church in its whole history, and it can often be instructive to us today as we compare our church with the biblical standard. The church is imperfect, and it is important to be able to assess the true state of the church in our own day. John Calvin in this area, as in so many others, can help us. He not only was a Reformer of the church, but in several of his writings he explained the character and need of reform in his days.

Near the beginning of his career as a Reformer, when he was only twenty-six, Calvin wrote the first edition of his *Institutes of the Christian Religion* in 1536. One of the reasons he wrote it was to explain to the world what he taught as a Reformer and to show that it was biblical. His introductory letter for this work was addressed to King Francis of France as a defense of the Reformation.

A few years later, when he was thirty, Calvin wrote a second defense of the Reformation. This one was particularly personal. He had served as a pastor in the newly Reformed church in the Swiss city of Geneva about twenty months, from 1536 to 1538, and was then exiled by the city council for pressing his vision of a disciplined church. He traveled to Strasbourg, then a German-speaking city, and was made pastor of a French-speaking congregation, working with the great Reformer there, Martin Bucer.

Cardinal Jacopo Sadoleto, a distinguished humanist scholar, thought that Geneva might be lured back to the old church. So, in 1538, he wrote an appeal to the Genevans to return to the church of their fathers, the church supported by history, now that they no longer followed the rebel Reformers who were only motivated by ambition and avarice. While the rulers of Geneva were not moved by Sadoleto's appeal, they wanted a strong defense of the Reformed religion to answer him. They concluded that only Calvin could write that answer. So the ones who had exiled him now appealed to him to defend them. He wrote a brilliant defense of the Reformation, in which he was remarkably passionate and personal because the attacks of Sadoleto were so personal. Here he presented clearly his views on justification and the authority of the Bible in the life of the church.

Because the *Reply to Cardinal Sadoleto* is relatively well known and accessible, we will not spend more time introducing it.[1] By contrast, Cal-

---

1 Those who would like to read more on Calvin's *Reply to Cardinal Sadoleto* may consult, for example, my book *John Calvin: Pilgrim and Pastor* (Wheaton, Ill.: Crossway, 2009).

vin's treatise *The Necessity of Reforming the Church* is less well known and requires a clear understanding of the situation in which it was written. Precisely because it has a different character and perspective from other writings of Calvin, it can also encourage us to look at the church in our day from a different perspective.

The Necessity of Reforming the Church was written in 1544. At that time, Calvin was a relatively young man, about thirty-five. He was a pastor in Geneva and had already established himself as a fine theologian, one of the most talented of what we might call the second-generation Reformers. Luther was still alive (he died in February 1546) and still a powerful presence in the life of the Reformation. So, at this point, he was still very much a presence and a power. Still, it was Calvin, not Luther, who was asked to write this defense of the Reformation, perhaps just because he was not so well known as Luther in Germany.

The invitation to write this treatise came to Calvin from Martin Bucer, the great first-generation Reformer of Strasbourg who had come to appreciate Calvin's talents during his years of exile in that city. Calvin was to write this treatise for a very special occasion: a meeting of the Diet of the Holy Roman Empire, which was to be held in the city of Speyer with Emperor Charles V present. The treatise would be addressed to the emperor as an explanation for the actions of his Protestant subjects in reforming the church. Calvin, in writing the treatise, was clearly aware of the political, religious, and legal issues troubling Europe and Germany in particular.

Politically, things were extraordinarily complicated in Europe. In 1544, the two greatest political powers in Europe were at war with each other: Emperor Charles V and King Francis I of France. This was a frequently recurring problem because Charles ruled not only the Holy Roman Empire—roughly Germany and Austria—but also the Netherlands and Spain and a significant part of Italy. These lands formed a ring of wealth and power in Europe with France at the center of the circle. So France often felt threatened, though France had the advantage of being a single, united country. Though Charles' lands were vast, he had the disadvantage of their being very spread out. All these various lands had their own traditions, their own politics, their own ways of behaving, and their own languages. They all wanted Charles to live with them and sometimes resisted his will when he was absent from them. He had huge problems of governance.

In 1543, a new war broke out in which France was so desperate that Francis made a military alliance with the Turkish sultan Suleiman the Magnificent. This outraged Europe—a Christian king had allied himself with the Muslim ruler who was constantly threatening Europe. Suleiman had already overrun Hungary and had actually threatened Vienna. Europe was threatened in a very serious way, and the king of France had made an alliance with this man against the Holy Roman emperor.

Religiously, Charles was facing the growth of Lutheranism in the empire, particularly in Germany. There were by 1544 significant numbers of territories that had become Lutheran, and Lutheranism seemed to keep growing. Charles was very upset about this. He apparently never seriously thought about Protestantism as an option. He was a traditional, rather pious Roman Catholic, and so he was convinced that the Roman church was the true church and that these Protestant heretics needed to be suppressed.

These political and religious dynamics came together in 1544 at the Diet of Speyer. A diet was roughly like a parliament; it was a gathering of princes and leaders of various territories and cities. The great power of a diet rested in its authority to approve new taxes and to raise troops for the imperial army. As Charles was in the midst of war with great enemies to the east and to the south, he was desperate for money and troops. (In those days, princes could not print money and needed real money to pay for troops and provisions.) The Lutheran princes knew he was desperate, and that meant they had leverage. They could force the emperor to discuss the religious situation and its future at the diet.

Earlier diets had discussed religion, most notably the Diet in Speyer in 1526, where the Protestants had first gotten their name. They offered a protestation to the emperor, and they became known as Protestants. They were granted at that time a measure of toleration. The game they played at these diets would go something like this: The emperor would accuse them of being heretics, and the Protestants would respond by saying that such a serious charge needed to be heard at a general council of the church. The emperor would then agree to delay any action against them until the ruling of a council if they would vote him taxes and troops. The situation was the same at Speyer in 1544. The Protestants wanted toleration and the emperor did not want to grant it. But he was willing to grant temporary toleration until the meeting of a general council in order to get money and troops to fight the French and the Turks.

This setting for Calvin's treatise was crucial because it very much influenced how he wrote it. As we look at the treatise, it is important to note that Calvin was not being asked to explain the whole of the Reformation. He was being asked to write to the German rulers who were laymen, not to theologians or ministers or priests or bishops. He was not being asked to offer a closely reasoned biblical exegesis or theological argument. He was being asked to lay out the case for why the church needed to be reformed without delay.

Near the beginning of the treatise, he said that he was directing his defense to the moderates. We must wonder if he smiled when he wrote that, because by 1544 there were not very many moderates left. Sixteenth-century Germany was very polarized. You had the Roman Catholics on the one side and the Lutherans on the other, and most of them were pretty convinced of their point of view. Still, Calvin was trying to show a desire to be reasonable, to address anybody who might be willing to face the reality of problems in the church. To do that, he laid out a case on the most obvious issues. He talked about things that laymen would notice. It is very important to bear that in mind. It was a very deliberate strategy that he pursued, and this strategy is something that we can apply to our own time.

Calvin divided his treatise into three parts. First, he looked at the present evils of the church, and then he looked at the remedies the Protestants had introduced in their churches, and then he looked at the reason they had made those changes without waiting for any approval from emperor, pope, or council. In each of these parts, Calvin examined four topics: worship, salvation, sacraments, and church government.

Calvin called these four topics the soul and body of the church. The soul of the church, Calvin said, is what makes it alive. What is the difference between a living body and a corpse? Calvin would have said "a soul." When the soul leaves, the body becomes a corpse. And the life-giving element of the church is worship and salvation. And the body, then, the instrument through which the soul works, is the sacraments and the government of the church.

Worship

We usually think of the Reformation as so much about the authority of the Bible and about salvation that it comes as a surprise that Calvin in this treatise said worship is the number one issue of the Christian religion. But he is reminding us that salvation is not an end in itself. It is a means to an end. What is the end for which we are saved? The end for which we are saved is to have a relationship with God. In glory, we will have unbroken fellowship with God, but for now public worship is one of the most important expressions of our fellowship with God. Calvin was right to insist that our worship must be honoring to God. He saw the worship of the Roman Catholic Church in which he had been raised as an utter betrayal of biblical standards of worship. For example, he observed that in such worship, half of God's glory was taken away from Him and distributed to various saints.

Calvin argued that the Roman Catholic Mass had become entirely a matter of ceremony. Every action, every element of the ceremony had a meaning, a justification, that people may or may not have understood. He concluded that these ceremonies were theatrical, showy, exhibitionist. He saw that the Mass had become theater, and we know the character of the theater is entertainment.

Now, entertainment can come in a variety of forms. We can be entertained by what is exuberant and boisterous, which tends to be the entertainment we have in our time, but entertainment can also be solemn and inspiring and moving. That is what Calvin saw in the Mass. People were coming to the ceremonies not to be drawn to God but to be entertained by a moving spectacle. If we share Calvin's indignation, we must then pause to ask to what extent much conservative Protestant worship in our time has become entertainment. How much of it is meant to be entertaining rather than drawing us to God? How much of it is intended to make God more acceptable to man rather than making man more acceptable to God? Do we really gather to meet with God according to His Word?

Calvin contended rather remarkably that the way to know how to meet with God is to listen to God. Here is what he said:

> Therefore, if we want Him to approve our worship, we must carefully keep this law that He enforces with utmost severity. The reason is twofold that the Lord, by forbidding and condemning all man-made worship, calls us back to obedience to His voice alone. For (1) this greatly applies to establishing His authority, so that we may not serve our own wills but rely entirely on His will, and (2) we are so proud that, if freedom is left to us, we can do nothing but go astray.

God wants to establish His authority and keep us from going astray, and He accomplishes those things by telling us how to worship Him. So often today we hear about the importance of liberty. We are free to do what we want in worship. God is just so happy to have us there that He does not care what we do. Now, nobody says it quite that boldly, but that is close to what we hear today in many circles. "I want to be happy, God wants me to be happy, and so I should feel good when I go to church." God does not want freedom in worship; He wants faithfulness. Calvin said, "This is so difficult to persuade the world of: God disapproves of all worship that has been established beyond His Word." God wants to be worshiped the way He tells us to worship Him. That surely seems reasonable.

Calvin stated this in several different ways. He wrote:

> Moreover, we have said that the Word of God is the sign that distinguishes the true worship of God from what is full of vice and evil. From this it is quickly concluded that the whole form

of worshiping God that is used in the world today is nothing but mere corruption. For they are not even concerned about what God has commanded or what He approves so that they may obey as it is fitting. Instead, they give themselves a license to devise worship that they later indulge to obey in place of God. Although I may seem to go beyond measure in saying that it must be done, let all works with which the world decides that they may worship God nevertheless be shaken off. With the generous exception of 10 percent, all were born rashly in the minds of people. Why do we want more? God despises, condemns, and curses all invented forms of worship. The bridle of God's Word pierces us to keep us in simple obedience.

Such statements are really strong. God curses fictitious worship. But Calvin continued: "But it does not escape my notice how difficult it is to persuade the world of this: God rejects and even hates whatever is devised by human reason for His worship." People will perform diffi-cult acts of external worship as long as they do not have to engage their hearts: "For although it is necessary for true worshipers of God to bring forth heart and soul, people always want to invent a manner of serving God that is entirely different from that, so that rendering service of the body to Him, they keep their soul for themselves." So, we will kneel, or bow, or stand as long as in our core God leaves us alone, as long as we do not actually have to meet with Him, as long as we do not have to go through the difficulty of opening our minds and hearts to His Word and being changed by His Word.

Calvin then offered a very concrete example. He said at the very heart of worship is prayer. Now, prayer arguably is the hardest thing we do in public worship. Once you have closed your eyes and folded your hands, it is very easy for the mind to just wander off. It is hard work really to pray with the minister as he is praying, and it tests the extent to which we are actually meeting with God. But it is also one of the most intimate ways that we meet with God. We are baring our souls to God. Do we believe He is there to hear us? If we do not pray, maybe we are saying we really do not believe He is actually with us. And Calvin said that is contrary to everything we find in the Scriptures. So, Calvin uses prayer as one of the tests of what our worship really amounts to in terms of glorifying God.

What is our worship really like? Are we meeting with God? Are we sensing that God deserves the glory? Do we understand that we are coming into His awesome presence and that we are there to praise Him, to speak to Him, and then to listen as He speaks to us? Do we want Him in all our worship to direct us by His Word? Here is the true character and the great simplicity of worship: God speaks and we respond.

Salvation

After considering worship, Calvin then turned to the matter of salvation. He argued that the church in his day was doing a terrible job of understanding what the Word of God really teaches about salvation. The first point he made in this section of the treatise is that the church was not taking sin seriously enough. He argued that too often we are content with a superficial analysis of sinfulness. Stealing, murder, adultery—those are our sins. But those are things that can be controlled more than the really profound sins—pride, hatred, enmity against others and against God. These are the elements of sin that he said the church was not calling on people to examine.

He expanded on this point by focusing on the doctrine of original sin, which he argued was being perverted or ignored. Here we might ask how well the church in our day is doing in proclaiming this doctrine. How often does the church today teach that every person is born in sin, alienated from God, guilty and corrupt? We must understand the reality and depths of human sin and evil.

In light of the seriousness of the problem of sin, Calvin said that we must see clearly that Christ has done everything for us in our salvation. He has accomplished all the work that needs to be done for us to be saved. Today, as in Calvin's day, churches are not always teaching that Christ is all our salvation. The message too often is that Christ has done everything He can do for us, and that we must now do our part to complete our salvation. Such a view makes the sinner's action, not Christ's, ultimately the determinative factor in salvation. Such teaching is false and deprives Him of the glory due to Him for His work.

In this section of the treatise, Calvin stressed that Christ is our only Priest. Calvin would certainly have agreed with Peter that all Christians are priests (1 Peter 2:9). But here he was insisting that there is no separate caste of priests who stand between God and man in the new covenant. There were priests who fulfilled that function in the old covenant. There was then a temple, and there were parts of that temple that could only be entered by priests. The average worshiper had to allow the priest to stand between him and God. Only the priest could enter the Holy Place and put the showbread before God, light the candles before God, and burn incense at the altar of incense in the Holy Place. Only a priest could offer a sacrifice on the altar for burnt offerings. Calvin emphasized that no such priesthood exists in the church. Christ is our only Priest, meaning that only He can do the priestly work that has to be done of offering a sacrifice to atone for sin.

The church in Calvin's day was full of priests, and priests clearly stood between man and God. The priests were the only ones who could enter through the rail to approach the altar, and their ministry at the altar was essential to salvation. Calvin was attacking that whole system of priests standing between God and man and was saying that the only priest between God and man is Christ our Savior. He is the only sacrifice, and He is the only sacrificer. He offered Himself once for all on the cross as the full and final payment for sin.

A related issue that Calvin was implicitly attacking was the Roman doctrine that priests offer the sacrifice of Christ on the altars of their churches. Any such notion is unbiblical and distracts from the unique priesthood of Christ.

We need to understand that we are saved by the grace of Christ alone. It seems amazing that such teaching could be controversial, and yet today in many churches the teaching is more man-centered than Christ-centered. We must recapture the great teaching of the Bible and the Reformation on the saving work of Christ.

Calvin moved from the work of Christ to the character of faith. Faith was very important to Calvin, and he always stressed that faith should be firm and confident. He was reacting sharply to so much of medieval religion, which was predicated on the notion that it is good for the people of God to be fearful and doubting. If you are fearful and uncertain about your relationship to God, you will try harder. Calvin was adamant that this turned the Christian religion on its head. God wants you to be confident that if you truly believe in Christ, you are His child and He loves you. Out of that relationship will flow the life that you ought to live before Him. It is not fear and doubt that drive the Christian life, Calvin said; it is confidence and assurance that motivate the Christian life. Knowing that we belong to God in Christ should lead us to an eager pursuit of God in worship and living for God in all of life.

If we are using Calvin's treatise as a mirror for today, we might ask whether many conservative Protestants wrestle with a great deal of doubt and fear. The answer is probably no. In fact, we may have just the opposite problem, that of presuming on God for faith and confidence. The answer to presumption is not doubt but true faith. Calvin would say that we are not saved by believing that we are saved. Rather, true faith is recognizing our need and looking away from ourselves to Christ and really trusting His work for us.

Having laid down these three key elements—sin, Christ, and faith—Calvin wrote surprisingly little about justification explicitly. He clearly stated that we are justified by mere gratuitous favor—that is, we are justified only by the gracious favor of God, not by anything we bring to God. If we understand sin, Christ, and faith correctly, we will certainly understand justification.

Calvin then turned to address some specific serious errors taught in his day related to the doctrine of salvation. He focuses on two evils in particular. The first evil is believing in free will. The doctrine of free will fails to understand the seriousness of sin and undermines the completeness of the work of Christ. Calvin insisted that this doctrine is evil and must be removed from the life of the church. Would we today follow Calvin in so passionately rejecting free will? Do we agree that free will endangers the gospel and the life of God's people?

One of the developments of American Christianity in the nineteenth and twentieth centuries was that conservative Protestants became so concerned about evangelism—which is a very good concern—that they were willing to make all sorts of compromises so Protestants could cooperate. So, free will adherents and free will critics often put that division aside so they could do evangelism together. Calvin would say that we must not do that. We would betray the gospel and evangelism.

A second great evil is thinking that we are justified by our own works or by our own merit. Calvin then paused and said, "Here we are not disputing about good works—whether they need to be supplied by the godly, are accepted by God, or have a reward before Him." Then he quoted Luther. He quoted Luther about five or six times in this treatise, and he did that very deliberately because Luther was still alive. Most of the Protestants at the diet thought of themselves as Lutherans, and he wanted to make the point that Protestants were standing together there. Luther too had said that there will of course be works in the life of a Christian. But he went on to say, as Calvin did, that those works will always need to be forgiven because they are always going to be somewhat contaminated by sin, and those works will never be pure enough to merit anything from God. Any reward we receive for our works, Calvin said, depends not "on their merit or worth but rather on the mere kindness of God." Our works are never so pure as to deserve God's reward. Rather, even our good works are the gift of God.

For Calvin, the truths of the doctrine of salvation are part of the very soul of the church. Do we see the soul of the church in the same way today? Have we failed to uphold faithfully the biblical doctrines?

Sacraments

The life of the church and of individual Christians in Calvin's day and in the Middle Ages revolved around the sacraments, and Rome had declared in the Middle Ages that there were seven sacraments. Two of those sacraments we as Protestants still recognize as instituted by Christ in the Scripture: baptism and the Lord's Supper. But Rome had declared that five other activities of the church were also sacraments, and this is important because for Rome, grace operates through the sacraments. It is primarily through the sacraments that a Roman Catholic receives the grace of God. Therefore, it is important to know which activities of the church are sacraments and which are not, and this became complicated in the Middle Ages because there were so many ceremonies.

Calvin said that the particular danger of the Roman Catholic view of the sacraments is that they become superstitious, as if the sacraments alone are sufficient for salvation. That's what a lot of Roman Catholics came to believe. Instead of bringing the worshiper to Christ, the sacraments easily became a replacement for Christ.

The foundational sacrament is baptism. Baptism is the entrance into the church. To this day in the Roman Catholic Church, you are not baptized in the sanctuary; you are baptized outside the church, often in the foyer but sometimes even in a separate building called a baptistery. This arrangement is a visual statement that you are not part of the church until you have been baptized. Ordinarily, if you are not baptized, you cannot be saved.

Baptism is so essential to salvation that during the Middle Ages, when infant mortality rates were very high, midwives were allowed to baptize infants in extreme circumstances. Baptism is then the only sacrament that does not have to be administered by a priest. It should ideally be administered by a priest, but it does not have to be because it is so vital.

Other sacraments follow. Confirmation seals you as an adult in the life of the church. The sacrament of reconciliation or penance involves your being forgiven by the priest for your sins after contrition, confession, and satisfaction. This sacrament in a sense is a restoration of baptism. Baptism washed away sin, and when sins are later committed they are washed away again by penance.

Then there are three sacraments that relate to particular changes in life. The first is the sacrament of marriage. Since marriage is sacramental, it cannot ordinarily be ended by divorce. The second sacrament in this category is ordination or holy orders, where you are made a priest. The recipient of this sacrament receives grace to perform his calling. The third sacrament here is the anointing of the sick, traditionally called the last rites. This sacrament washes away sin at the end of life and prepares for death.

These sacraments were at the center of the life of the church in Calvin's day, and they still are today for Roman Catholics. But there is one more sacrament to consider, the most important one. That sacrament is the Eucharist or the Lord's Supper. In the medieval era, the regular experience of going to church was centered on seeing the miraculous work of the priest at the altar changing the bread and wine into the very body and blood of Christ and offering Christ to God as a propitiatory sacrifice, and on bowing to worship the consecrated host. Actually receiving the elements of the Eucharist became secondary. Many people came to see the miracle of the Mass as performed by the priest and then left. This practice became so troubling to church authorities that the Fourth Lateran Council in 1215 adopted a rule that every Roman Catholic has to receive the Eucharist at least once a year during the Easter season.

Calvin rightly saw the sacraments as the body of the church, as one of the places where the soul of religion—worship and salvation—touched people the most. Because of their importance, the meaning of the sacraments had to be closely examined. Are they biblical? Does Scripture in fact teach that the sacraments automatically confer grace on the recipient? Unsurprisingly, Calvin said the Roman church's teachings were not right.

According to Calvin, five of Rome's seven sacraments are complete human inventions. Adding sacraments that Christ did not establish in the Bible is disobedience to God and a misunderstanding of the purpose and character of sacraments. Calvin, along with Luther and all the other Reformers, said that when you look carefully at the Word of God, only baptism and the Lord's Supper are instituted by Christ as sacraments.

What is a sacrament? Calvin and others embraced a very simple definition derived from Augustine in the ancient church: a sacrament is a visible sign of invisible grace. So, the idea of a sacrament is linked to the idea of grace. But what is the linkage? What is the relationship of the sign to the thing signified? The sign of baptism is water, and water carries with it something of the message of the sacrament, because water is inherently associated with washing. So there is a connection between the sign and what it points to. With the Lord's Supper, the sign clearly is the bread and the wine that are established by our Lord, and they point to the idea that the Lord must nourish His people. Baptism has a kind of once-for-all character to it; you are washed once at the beginning of your Christian experience. Then, the Lord's Supper is the ongoing nurturing of the people of God through the sign of the Lord's Supper.

Calvin said that when the sacraments are rightly understood, they point to Christ, but when the sacraments are incorrectly understood, they actually become a wall between us and Christ. That happened in the Middle Ages. The people looked at the water of baptism and said, "That water saves!" They looked at the bread and wine of the Lord's Supper and said, "That bread and wine nourish us!" Calvin insisted that this fails to understand the teaching of Jesus. The sign of washing in water points to and promises Christ who truly washes us. The sign of bread and wine points to and promises Christ who truly feeds us. If the bread becomes entirely the body of Christ, then there would be no sign of grace but only the reality of grace. The sacrament would not point to Christ but would be Christ. The effect of such teaching is to take us away from Christ.

If we try to carry Calvin's thinking into our own day, we would ask ourselves how important sacraments are to us. Among Protestants today, we do find some discussion of baptism, but the discussion almost always is about who ought to be baptized. Should we baptize only believers, or should we baptize believers and their children? Once we have settled that question in our minds, we hardly ever think about baptism again. But baptism really ought to be a continuing reality in the life of the Christian. It should constantly testify to us that we belong to Christ and have a new, cleansed life in Him.

Baptism is an indelible sign. It is a sign that Christ places on His own that says, "These are Mine." Does that mean baptism automatically or mechanically saves you? No. Baptism is a promise, a visible promise from God of His gospel. And because we are weak, because sometimes we forget promises that are made just to our ears, God also makes promises to our eyes and promises that we can feel. Baptism brings that promise to us.

Luther, who wrestled with periods of spiritual doubt, would often repeat to himself: "I am baptized. I am baptized." Somebody said to him once, "How do you know you're a Christian?" He said, "I have been baptized." That can be a good or a bad answer depending on what you mean by it. If you mean, "I've had water sprinkled on me, so God is stuck with me," that is a bad answer. But if you mean, "God made a promise so personally to me that it touched me in the water of baptism, and when I am troubled with doubts, I remember that in the water of baptism Christ made a promise to me," then that is a good answer.

The Lord's Supper is the sacrament of ongoing promise and encouragement. The Lord's Supper says to us, "You need your whole life to be fed and encouraged with the body and blood—the person and work—of Christ," and the bread and the wine say, "God gives to you the body and blood of Christ as your salvation." In the Lord's Supper, God comes to us in the bread and wine with a promise that as surely as we eat this bread and drink this wine, so surely are the body and blood of Christ our food to eternal life. Do we today value the sacraments as we ought for the blessing they are to us?

Are we in any danger of inventing sacraments in our day as the medieval church did in its day? If there is one sacrament we have tended to invent in our own time, it is the sacrament of music. In many churches, there is an awful lot of time spent singing to bring us close to God. Music can be very helpful and very powerful, but it is not a sacrament. Music is not primarily God's movement to us, which is what sacraments do, but music is our movement to God, bringing our prayers, our thanks, our glorification to Him.

Church Government

In the history of the church, Protestants have debated a great deal about church government. We even name our denominations after church government. There are Congregationalists, who think the congregation governs the church. There are Presbyterians, who think elders govern the church. And there are Episcopalians, who think bishops govern the church.

We might expect John Calvin in this section of the treatise to discuss the role of bishops in the life of the church and particularly the role of the pope, the bishop of Rome. What an ideal opportunity to attack the claims of the bishop of Rome to universal sovereignty over the whole church. Surprisingly, he did not do that. In talking about church government, he really talked about the role of ministers. What should the work of ministers be? What is the function of clergy in the life of the church?

That question is actually very important. It is valuable to discuss whether we ought to have bishops and whether there should be a pope in the life of the church. But even if you believe in a pope and bishops, they are mostly removed from the life of the average Christian. Most Roman Catholics have never met the pope, and they even go a long time without seeing their bishop. Calvin argued that what is really important is the clergy as they function in the local church. Calvin asked, What is their function? What ought they be doing? What is the role that God assigned to them?

Calvin argued vigorously that the prime calling of the clergy is to edify the people of God with the Word of God. He defended this teaching by quoting a number of ancient Christian authors who said the same thing. The Reformers wanted to demonstrate that they were not presenting brand-new teachings. They insisted that they were simply reforming the church according to the Word of God and interpreting the Bible as the fathers of the church had done for centuries.

The preaching of the Word had been at the very center of the life of the church for centuries. When you go back to the ancient church, you see the centrality of preaching in Christian worship. But as time went on, preaching began to die out, in part due to declining education among the clergy. Priests in the Middle Ages, particularly in rural areas, were very poorly educated. Many of them could not read. It is impossible to study the Bible and prepare a sermon if you cannot read. They could instead simply memorize the Canon of the Mass. As the church more and more became focused on sacraments and on ceremonies, the importance of preparing preachers declined in the mind of the church.

Now, Bible reading had always been a part of the worship of the church, but it happened that it was often the same passages read over and over again and very often in languages people did not understand. It is not helpful if you do not understand Latin or you do not understand Old Church Slavonic to have the Bible read in those languages. That was why one of the great commitments of the Reformation was to have services in the language of the people. The Word has to be comprehensible. We have to hear what God is saying to us. That was at the very heart of the Reformation.

The commitment of the Reformation to the Word led to a rigorous education for the ministers. As a result, the Protestant clergy in the sixteenth and seventeenth centuries were probably the best-educated clergy in the history of the church. Education was strongly emphasized so that ministers would be able to preach the Word of God. That is why historically in Protestant education for ministers, the biblical languages of Greek and Hebrew have been studied extensively, so that ministers could read the Word of God in the original languages and help the people of God really understand it. Unfortunately, too often today we have gotten away from that rigorous education, and as a result the Protestant clergy are much less able to faithfully minister the Word.

The sad reality is that when it comes to choosing a pastor, the church in our day might not be so different from the church in Calvin's day. There are a lot of people who go to church for the show, and it does not matter if the minister really knows the Word. What matters is this: Is he a good entertainer? Can he tell a good story? Can he tell a good joke? Or are people today clamoring for the Word of God? Do very many people leave church saying, "I did not hear enough of the Word of God"?

Calvin next discussed the holiness required of preachers and of the leaders of the church. He said three great sins had beset the clergy of his time: pride, cruelty, and sexual immorality. There has been some discussion about what has promoted the sad scandals in the Roman Catholic Church in our day with priests and their sexual immorality. As a solution to this problem, some have talked about ending celibacy as a practice for Roman Catholic clergy. But the real problem in the Roman church is not celibacy. It is the priesthood. It is the very fact that these people think they are set apart and, by being set apart, holy. The conviction that ordination makes the priest holy can contribute to a mind-set where a priest imagines that he is so special that his sins do not matter. Instead, a minister, just like every Christian, must mortify sin and pursue holiness in a serious and persevering way.

Calvin was also concerned about the tendency of leaders in the church to become tyrannical. He defined tyranny as the claim of the church to make laws that everybody has to keep under threat of eternal loss and yet that have no warrant in the Word of God. For instance, does the church have a right to forbid eating meat during Lent? Calvin said absolutely not. That is tyranny. It is laying down rules that God has not asked His people to keep. Only God through His Word may govern the life of God's people. Protestantism stands for Christian freedom from men's ideas and men's practices so that we can be free to follow God according to His Word.

We can see how church government, which might seem at first glance like a peripheral issue, is a critical issue for the people of God. It has to do with the question of authority in the life of the church. What is the authority that a minister has? The ministers have no authority in themselves. They have authority only to teach the Word of God. Tyrannical authority not only violates the freedom God has given Christians, but by undermining the Word of God it undermines our spiritual health.

In Calvin's day, people had only limited involvement in the choice of their ministers. In our day, we have great influence on the choice of our ministers. So we have to be willing to take the responsibility to say: What do I want? Who am I looking for? Who am I encouraging in the opening of the Word of God? We must seek godly, faithful ministers.

The Need for Action

The first 55 percent of Calvin's treatise covers the areas in which reform was required, and the last 45 percent covers how that reform was to be carried out. Some of this material is less immediately applicable to our day because Calvin lived in such a radically different world from our own. But it still raises a critical question: How do we go about improving the church in our day?

Calvin wrote: "The question is whether the diseases [in the church] are the sort that attention to them may not bear longer delay, so that it is neither useful nor permitted to wait for remedies that are too slow. We are accused of rashness and wicked innovation because we have dared to move anything at all in the church from its former condition." Then he said that he planned to "show from the matter itself that we did not rush before the time was right, did nothing rashly, did nothing outside our duty, and did nothing unless we were driven by utmost necessity." God's glory was being compromised. Christ's salvation was being obfuscated. The sacraments had been completely distorted and corrupted. Ministers were not doing their work. Calvin said the Reformers had to act.

Critics of the Reformers complained that they had acted too violently. That, Calvin insisted, was simply untrue. Luther had begun gently, Calvin said: "When Luther emerged in the beginning, he lightly noted (and that with moderation) only a few abuses—both excessively crass ones and ones no longer tolerable—more so that he might indicate that he desired them to be corrected than dare to correct them himself. This immediately sounded a call to arms from the enemy, and when the tension was raised more and more, our enemy thought that this was the best solution: to suppress the truth with force and brutality." Calvin was right. There was an effort to destroy the Reformation movement right from the beginning. And Calvin noted that we should not be surprised about that. In the whole history of the church, wherever truth has been proclaimed, it has caused commotion because those who oppose the truth stand against it.

In the letter of Jude we read: "Beloved, although I was very eager to write to you about our common salvation, I found it necessary to write appealing to you to contend for the faith that was once for all delivered to the saints" (v. 3). This verse is seminal. Jude declares that the whole Apostolic faith was delivered to the saints in the first century. The faith does not evolve or develop over centuries. The faith does not get supplemented by new traditions.

Further, Jude wrote: "But you must remember, beloved, the predictions of the apostles of our Lord Jesus Christ. They said to you, 'In the last time there will be scoffers, following their own ungodly passions.' It is these who cause divisions, worldly people, devoid of the Spirit" (vv. 17–19). Who causes divisions in the church? Somehow, those who uphold biblical teaching often are accused of causing divisions. But who always causes divisions according to Jude? Divisions are caused by worldly people who want to change the church to suit their own passions. Calvin may well have had Jude in mind as he justified the work of the Reformers. Things were so bad that they had to be changed.

Then Calvin addressed the charge that the Reformers had made things worse in the church. Calvin rejected that utterly, saying their efforts had borne good fruit in the lives of the people:

> I leave unmentioned the correction of outward idolatry and very many superstitions and errors, which must not be regarded as nothing. But is this really no fruit—that many truly godly people relate that, after they received us, they learned how to worship God with a pure heart at last? That they began to invoke Him with a peaceful conscience? That, freed from constant torments, they took in a true taste of Christ, in whom they found rest? But if proofs are sought that are evident in the sight of men, it does not go so badly with us that we are not able to boast in very many. How many people, although they were previously characterized by a more corrupt life, so repented that they appeared to have been converted into new people?

Closely related to the claim that the Reformation had made the church worse was the charge that the Reformers were guilty of schism. Schism is the sin of unnecessary and inappropriate division in the life of the church. The history of the church shows that there has always been commotion and division in the life of the church. And Calvin's response again was that the Reformers had not left the church. Those who had deserted Christ, those who had deserted His Word, had left the church.

What, then, was the path to reforming the church? Calvin acknowledged that several ways to reform had been proposed. The first was to submit all questions to the judgment of the pope. You will not be surprised that Calvin did not find this a useful solution. He said the pope was a tyrant, and a relatively recent tyrant at that. The pope had really only had tyranny in the church for about four hundred years. Since the pope was in a sense the biggest problem, you could not expect him to solve the problem. Further, Calvin said, "When everything was still intact, Luther humbly asked the pontiff to convince himself to heal the very severe diseases of the church." Luther was willing to submit to the pope if he would lead the reform, and the pope refused. So this was no avenue forward.

Calvin also addressed the question whether a universal or ecumenical council of the church should be convened to solve the problem. Protestants, especially Lutherans, had been suggesting that for years. The pope did not want a council because he was afraid he could not control a council. A century earlier, councils had gotten completely out of control, and the popes were exceedingly nervous about a council lest history repeat itself. But Calvin said the Reformers could not be assured that a council would do the right thing if it would not submit to the Word of God. So, Calvin said it would be expedient to start locally and regionally in Germany, to get leaders of the church together around the Bible and figure out how to move forward. In a sense, that was in part what the Diet at Speyer was actually doing. It was functioning as a regional council to think about religious things, and the pope was furious. He did not want any religious issues being discussed regionally without his authorization and supervision.

The church in Calvin's day was huge, was united around the pope and the bishops, was wealthy, influential, and powerful, and was closely connected to the civil government. Most of the leaders of the old church had no interest in change. The emperor and the other Roman Catholics at Speyer showed no interest in Calvin's treatise. Although the church and the world today are very different from what they were in Calvin's day, we can still learn valuable lessons from Calvin's treatise on how to improve the church.

The essential lesson is very simple. The way to reform the church is to keep studying the Word of God and then to try to live it out. The Scriptures themselves repeatedly talk about the importance of the Word of God. When Paul was taking his leave of the Ephesian elders, he said, "And now I commend you to God and to the word of his grace, which is able to build you up and to give you the inheritance among all those who are sanctified" (Acts 20:32). Jesus said, "If you abide in my word, you are truly my disciples" (John 8:31). When Jesus was facing temptation, He turned to the Word, saying, "It is written, 'Man shall not live by bread alone, but by every word that comes from the mouth of God'" (Matt. 4:4).

There is nowhere else to go but to the Bible for us to know the will of God. We have to keep coming back to it. We see that approach commended in that familiar verse in Acts 17:11 when Paul goes to the Bereans and they are called noble because when they listened to Paul they compared everything they heard to the Word of God. Or we could go to Psalm 81: "Hear, O my people, while I admonish you! O Israel, if you would but listen to me!" (v. 8). The problem is not with the Word. The problem is with the listening. Psalm 81:11–13 is striking: "But my people did not listen to my voice; Israel would not submit to me. So I gave them over to their stubborn hearts, to follow their own counsels. Oh, that my people would listen to me, that Israel would walk in my ways!" Is it really unreasonable for the Lord to ask that His people would listen and walk in His ways? Does that seem like an unreasonable request from the Creator and Redeemer of His people? And yet, that seems to have been controversial through much of the history of the church.

We should be pursuing church unity. We should not be content to be seriously divided. We as Protestants are often too indifferent to the dividedness of the church. But the only way to achieve unity, the only way to overcome differences, is to look to Scripture and to study it and to do so not just as individuals but as the community of the church.

The New Testament letters always assume the responsibility of the whole Christian community to pursue the truth. One of the great evils in the Roman church is the tendency for members to say: "I do not have to know the truth. I do not have to study the Bible. It is enough that the priests study and the bishops study and the pope studies. I just believe what they tell me." That may sound pious, but there is not a hint of that attitude in the New Testament. The Apostle Peter wrote: "Simeon Peter, a servant and apostle of Jesus Christ, to those who have obtained a faith of equal standing with ours by the righteousness of our God and Savior Jesus Christ" (2 Peter 1:1). He was saying that we all have an equal standing before God in faith, and so we all have an equal responsibility to try to think these things through and not lay that responsibility on somebody else.

This is the way forward in reforming the church in our day—to invite people to study the Word on the matters about which we differ. If people will not study the Word, then that is a sign that that is not a good church. Reforming the church may mean changing churches. That can be a hard thing, but sometimes it is necessary. If you are not being fed by the Word of God, you need to be somewhere where you will be fed by the Word of God and encouraged to study the Word of God and to grow in the Word of God.

When the Apostle Paul reflected on his experience of suffering, he was told by God, "My power is made perfect in weakness" (2 Cor. 12:9). Nobody likes weakness. We do not want to be weak. We want to be strong. But Paul was saying that God's power is often better displayed in our weakness than in our strength. We as conservative Protestants in America have known a long season of a lot of strength, a long season of big churches and full churches and strong preachers and strong leaders. We have had many privileges, and maybe we will not always have those privileges. But we should not lose heart. God promises that His power will be made perfect in weakness.

We must hold on to the confidence that the only way forward is to stick with the Word. Calvin said that we can only preach the Word; God has to give the fruit. There are going to be times when there is great fruit and times when there is not so much fruit, times of great apparent success and times of not so much success. But our call is to be faithful. Our call is to love the Word. And together we will be growing in grace and we will be involved in the necessary reforming of the church.

TRANSLATOR'S NOTE

The works that are translated here had already been put into English quite ably by Henry Beveridge in the nineteenth century. Although his translations are becoming dated with the changes in the English language over the last two centuries, I often referred to them as I translated, both to avoid replication of his work and to ensure that I was staying on the right track. In any case, the versions before you are translated afresh from the Latin. I strove to present an essentially literal translation of Calvin so as to bring to modern-day readers, as much as possible, what Calvin intended to convey to his sixteenth-century audience. May readers forgive the translations for appearing stilted at times by remembering that they were initially letters to an emperor and a cardinal.

This translation is dedicated to my wife, Amy.

THE NECESSITY
OF REFORMING
THE CHURCH
(1544)

A Supplication
to the most invincible Caesar, Charles V,
the most illustrious princes, and other ranking officials,
now holding an assembly of the empire at Speyer,
to determine sincerely to address the concern
of reforming the church

Published in the name of all who want
Christ to reign

By John Calvin
1544

A Supplication
to the most invincible Caesar, Charles V,[1]
the illustrious princes, and other ranking officials:

This assembly was ordered by you, O Caesar Augustus. In it we are all deciding on the present condition of the church, which is most wretched and nearly regarded as lost. To correct it for the better, may you at last enter and settle on a method with the very distinguished princes of the empire and the other noblemen. Therefore, because you are now sitting down in a public assembly for this deliberation, on my knees I ask and beg of you first, O Caesar, and at the same time of you, O distinguished princes and noblemen, to read and weigh carefully what I am publishing in your midst, so that you may not feel troubled. It is the size and weight of the cause that should stir you up with eagerness to listen. But

---

1   Charles V (1500–1558) served as emperor of the Holy Roman Empire from 1519 to 1556. Calvin addresses him as "Caesar" throughout, harking back to the early Roman emperors. Only in the first sentence does Calvin call Charles "Caesar Augustus," after the first Roman emperor, who ruled from 27 BC to AD 14.

I am bringing the matter before your eyes, so that you may be able to determine easily what your part is. Whoever I may be, I profess that I am here supporting the protection of holy doctrine and the church. In this name I seem to deserve at least this one thing: that you do not deny me an audience, until it is apparent that either I falsely make use of such a title or faithfully display it and show in the matter itself that I bring before me. Moreover, although I know that I am by no means a match for such a burden, I nevertheless have no fear that, when the reason for my attendance has been heard by you, I will be accused of negligence or rashness because I have been bold to come to the aid of this magistracy. There are two matters about which people usually take action to commend or indeed to defend something. For we regard both what is done with sincere and godly devotion worthy of praise and what is expressed by public necessity as at least worthy of justification. Because both of these factors apply to me, I have no doubt, given your fairness, that I can easily defend this counsel of mine to you. For where better or more sincerely, where even at this time, is it allowed for me to devote myself in a matter more necessary than if I try to be present with my strength to the church of Christ, to which it is lawful to deny nothing at all and which is now struggling greatly and in extreme danger? Nevertheless, there is no reason to say much about myself in advance. Therefore, receive what I am saying as if one voice of all those who have already taken care to reform the church or who desire that it be restored to true order were shouting. There are several princes of the highest rank and many state officials present in this cause. I speak for all these in such a way that they all speak at the same time with one voice more truly through me. Add to these the infinite multitude of godly people who, scattered throughout various parts of the Christian world, nevertheless with common consent back me in this action. Finally, consider this the shared pleading of all who so seriously grieve over the present corruption of the church that they are no longer able to endure it and will not give up until they see some change. I know that we have been marked for infamy by hateful names. But by whatever name it may please you to call us at last, hear our cause in the meantime and then afterward judge in what place we should be regarded.

First of all, there is no question that the church struggles with many very terrible diseases. All people agree about this, even those who judge moderately. But the question is whether the diseases are the sort that attention to them may not bear longer delay, so that it is neither useful nor permitted to wait for remedies that are too slow. We are accused of rashness and wicked innovation because we have dared to move anything at all in the church from its former condition. What? Even if it was done reasonably and rightly? There are those—so I hear—who do not hesitate to condemn us even in this because they think that we should have desired correction but were not allowed to attempt it. From those people I desire to ask nothing else now except that they suspend judgment for a while until I show from the matter itself that we did not rush before the time was right, did nothing rashly, did nothing outside our duty, and did nothing unless we were driven by utmost necessity. In order to prove this, I will articulate the matters about which we contend.

When in the beginning God stirred up Luther and others who carried the torch before us to find the way of salvation, by whose ministry our churches were founded and established, we affirm that those heads of doctrine, in which the truth of our religion, the pure and lawful worship of God, and human salvation are contained, had been very nearly abolished. We affirm, moreover, that at that time the use of the sacraments had been marred and corrupted, and the government of the church had been turned into a form of ugly, unbearable tyranny. Perhaps these issues are not yet sufficiently prevalent to arouse certain people until they are expressed better. Therefore, I will do not so much what the subject requires as what my ability will allow. It is not my plan, however, to recount and examine every controversy. For that would require a long disputation for which there is now no place. I only want to set before you how righteous and necessary the causes were that compelled us to this change, which is being attributed to us as vice. This cannot be accomplished, however, unless I undertake three things at the same time. First, I must briefly mention the vices that urged us to seek remedies. Second, I must discuss how suitable and salutary were the very remedies that our people applied. Third, I must make clear how it was not permitted to delay with further hesitation, since the matter required immediate change. Because I only touch on that first matter to make way for the rest, I will try to touch on few things. In clearing up the crime of sacrilege, audacity, and sedition, with which we are burdened as if with unfavorable haste (we falsely acquired it, for it did not belong to our party), I will dwell on it longer.

If one should ask on what things Christianity chiefly stands among us and retains its truth, the following not only certainly hold first place but also comprehend under themselves all the remaining parts and to that degree the whole force of Christianity: that people may know (1) how God is rightly worshiped and (2) whence they must seek salvation for themselves. When these things are taken away, even if we boast the name of Christ, our profession is empty and useless. After these things follow the sacraments and the government of the church. Just as the latter were established for the preservation of the former doctrines, so they should not be applied to anything else, nor can they be judged from elsewhere (whether they are administered in a holy and orderly way or otherwise), except when they are considered for this end. Here is a clear and familiar analogy: the government in the church—the pastoral office and the rest of the orders—together with the sacraments represent the body; however, that doctrine which prescribes the rule for rightly worshiping God and which shows where people's consciences should place their trust for salvation represents the soul, which breathes into the body itself, rendering it alive and active, and preventing it from being a dead, useless corpse. What I have said so far is not under dispute among godly people of a right, sound mind.

Now let us define the lawful worship of God. Indeed, its chief foundation is to acknowledge Him just as He is—the only source of all virtue, righteousness, holiness, wisdom, truth, power, goodness, mercy, life, and salvation. It is, moreover, to attribute and assign the glory of all things entirely to Him, seeking all things in Him alone. Finally, it is, when we have any need, to lift it up to Him alone. Invocation is born from this, and from it flow praises and thanksgiving, which are testimonies of that glory that we attribute to Him. This is the true hallowing of His name, which He requires of us above all. Adoration is connected to this, by which we show to Him reverence that is worthy of His greatness and excellence. Ceremonies serve this, whether as props or means, so that the body may be exercised together with the soul in the profession of divine worship. The denial of ourselves follows next, so that renouncing the flesh and the world, we may be transformed unto the newness of mind. The purpose of this is that we may no longer live for ourselves but resign ourselves to Him to rule and lead us. Moreover, by this self-denial we are made ready for obedience and deference to His will, so that the fear of God may reign in our hearts and guide all the actions of our lives. These elements contain the true and sincere worship of God. The Holy Spirit approves of and delights in this alone, which He teaches everywhere in Scripture. The very notion of godliness teaches the same without a long disputation. Moreover, from the beginning there has been no other method for worshiping God than what this spiritual truth, which is plain and simple before us, entailed in types under the Old Testament. This is also what Christ's words mean in John 4, "The time has come when true worshipers will worship the Father in Spirit and in truth" (John 4:23). To be sure, with those words He did not mean to deny that worship had existed in that spiritual manner among the Patriarchs but only to indicate a distinction in outward form. For, although they had foreshadowed the Spirit with many types, it is simple among us. Otherwise, this always prevailed: it is necessary that God, who is Spirit, be worshiped in Spirit and in truth.

Therefore, the rule that distinguishes pure worship of God from its corrupted form is universal: we must not mix in what has seemed good to us but must observe what He requires who alone has the authority to command. Therefore, if we want Him to approve our worship, we must carefully keep this law that He enforces with utmost severity. The reason is twofold that the Lord, by forbidding and condemning all man-made worship, calls us back to obedience to His voice alone. For (1) this greatly applies to establishing His authority, so that we may not serve our own wills but rely entirely on His will, and (2) we are so proud that, if freedom is left to us, we can do nothing but go astray.

Moreover, once we have turned aside from the way, afterward there is no end as long as we are buried in a multitude of superstitions. Therefore, the Lord, so that He may claim the full right of lordship for Himself, rightly commands us to do what He wills, so that He refuses whatever humans have devised that is beyond His command. He also rightly does this because He blocks off limits for us with His mouth, lest by inventing corrupt worship, we provoke God's wrath toward us. This is so difficult to persuade the world of: God disapproves of all worship that has been established beyond His Word. Instead, this persuasion prevails and is as it were formed in the bones and marrow of all people: whatever they do they have sufficiently just approval for it, provided they display some zeal for the glory of God. But since God not only considers empty but also openly hates what we support for worshiping Him beyond His command, what do we profit by doing anything to the contrary? These are the clear and distinct words of God. Obedience is better than sacrifice (1 Sam. 15:22). He is worshiped in vain through the commandments of men (Matt. 15:9). Whatever is added to His Word is a lie, especially in regard to mere will-worship (ἐθελοθρησκείαν), which is emptiness. Once the judge has made a pronouncement, there is no longer any time for dispute.

Now, O Caesar, may your majesty and very distinguished princes consider me here and give me your attention. Today everything everywhere in which the Christian of the world puts the worship of God differs from this method. Indeed, in word they concede the glory of all goods to God, but in deed they concede only half or a majority to Him when they share His virtues with the saints. Let our enemies finish playing as they want. For they falsely accuse us of excessively magnifying their trivial errors, which they themselves do. Therefore, I will simply set forth the matter itself as it is clear to everyone. The offices of God have been distributed among the saints in such a way that they have been regarded as added to the Most High God by supporting His aims, in the multitude of which He lies hidden. To be sure, I am not complaining about anything other than what the whole world confesses in a popular proverb. Indeed, what do they mean when they say that the Lord was not known before the Apostles, except that the Apostles are raised to that height where the majesty of Christ is either covered over or at least made obscure? According to this wickedness, the world, having abandoned the living source, was instructed to dig scattered, open graves (Jer. 2:13). Indeed, where do they seek salvation and good, if not in God alone? But all common life openly cries out against this. For they say that they seek salvation and all goods in God. But since they seek these things elsewhere than in Him alone, a false pretext exists.

Vices will make the credibility of this matter manifest. The invocation of God was first corrupted in them, and then nearly overturned and extinguished. As we have said, by invocation people bear witness to whether they attribute glory to God. Therefore, from this it will also be possible to observe whether people transfer the glory due to Him to creatures. Indeed, for the invocation of God, more is required than prayer of any sort. That is to say, let the human soul certainly establish that it is God alone in whom it should take refuge, because He alone can help in time of need and has taken it upon Himself to do so. Moreover, no one can have that sense except the person who considers the command by which God calls us to Himself and the promise that He joins to the command about hearing our prayers. But the method of His command has not been observed, so that the masses have indiscriminately invoked angels and dead people at the same time as God. But if the wiser people were not invoking angels and people in the place of God, they were at least regarding them as mediators by whose intercession they might obtain what they were seeking. Where, therefore, was the promise at that time that was supported by the intercession of Christ alone? And so, abandoning the only mediator, Christ, everyone took himself to his own patrons whom he had made for himself. Or, if indeed place was given to Christ, He was nevertheless lying hidden, like some sheep in the midst of a flock.

Now, since nothing opposes the true invocation of God more than hesitation and lack of confidence, it has so taken hold that it has nearly been received as the law of praying rightly. But how did that happen? Well, the world did not understand why all those vices prevailed.

Moreover, people understand neither that God wants to be invoked by us and promises that He will do whatever we ask (trusting His command and promise), nor that He put forth Christ for us as an advocate in whose name our prayers may be favorably heard. For that reason, may the serious prayers that are held everywhere in the church be put away. To be sure, they will be found tainted by countless blemishes. Therefore, let judgment be made to what extent the worship of God has been corrupted in this matter. And yet there has been no less corruption in acts of thanksgiving. The public hymns bear witness to this, in which the praise for all goods is attributed to the saints as God's colleagues.

Now, what shall I say about adoration? Even when people want to show reverence to God, do they not want to do so with statues and images? To be sure, the person who thinks there is something to these things and to the madness of the heathens is in error. For God not only forbade us to adore stones but also to attribute a deity to them so that He may be adored in them. The heathens of old, to cover their wickedness, also once used the same pretexts that people bring forward today out of devotion to protect this abomination. Furthermore, it is agreed that the saints are also adored in the place of God, particularly their bones, clothes, shoes, and images. But some sophisticated person will object that there are different kinds of adoration. There is, they say, creaturely veneration (*dulia*) in which honor is given to saints, their images, and bones. There is also divine veneration (*latria*) reserved for God, fit for Him alone. Growing insane, people also invented a supreme form of creaturely veneration (*hyperdulia*) in which the blessed Virgin might be praised above others. But those are as it were subtle distinctions, whether they have been written down or have come into the minds of those who prostrate themselves before statues. In any case, the world is full of idolatry no less crass, no less palpable, so to speak, than what existed among the ancient Egyptians, which all the prophets condemned everywhere.

I am briefly touching on every matter because I will write more critically about them shortly. Now I come to ceremonies. Although they should be serious testimonies of the worship of God, they are instead mockeries of God. For, in addition, a new Judaism, which God had abolished with a clear voice, was stirred up again in place of Him. More-over, by gathering many childish follies here and there, they have also mixed in some ungodly rites and other profane things, which were put together more for a theatrical performance than for the majesty of our religion. This was the first sin: this great multitude of ceremonies that God had once and for all removed by His own authority was demanded again. Next, because ceremonies should coexist with the living practice of godliness, the world has many frivolous, useless customs with which it is uselessly occupied. To be sure, this is far deadlier than the plague because, in whatever ceremonies they have played with God, they think that they have been beautifully discharged and thus as if the whole force of godliness and worship of God were contained in them.

In regard to self-denial, on which regeneration to the newness of life depends, the whole doctrine was either entirely removed from the minds of people or was half-buried so that it was known to few and tenuously at that. But this is the spiritual sacrifice that the Lord commends above all: that, the old man having been put to death, we may be transformed into the new man. It may be possible that some preachers babble about those words. But the force of these things is not kept by them, from which it is established that they firmly contradict us because we are trying to restore this part of the worship of God. If they ever dispute about penance, which is special, they only draw on it contemptuously, mentioning it only in the external exercises of the body. As Paul testifies, such external exercises do not have much use (Col. 2:23; 1 Tim. 4:8). This perversion must be endured less, because the world truly strives after a shadow of a destructive error. While true repentance is ignored, they rush with their whole hearts into abstinences, vigils, et cetera—the empty principles of the world, as Paul calls them (Gal. 4:9).

Moreover, we have said that the Word of God is the sign that dis-tinguishes the true worship of God from what is full of vice and evil. From this it is quickly concluded that the whole form of worshiping God that is used in the world today is nothing but mere corruption. For they are not even concerned about what God has commanded or what He approves so that they may obey as it is fitting. Instead, they give themselves a license to devise worship that they later indulge to obey in place of God. Although I may seem to go beyond measure in saying that it must be done, let all works with which the world decides that they may worship God nevertheless be shaken off. With the generous exception of 10 percent, all were born rashly in the minds of people. Why do we want more? God despises, condemns, and curses all invented forms of worship. The bridle of God's Word pierces us to keep us in simple obedience. When, having shaken off the yoke, we wander over to our invented forms of worship and offer to Him what has been fabricated out of human rashness, however much they make us smile, they are empty trifles before Him; no, rather they are filthy pollutions. Advocates of human traditions have various beautiful colors with which they paint them. And Paul certainly confesses that an appearance of wisdom is visible in them (Col. 2:23). But because God makes more of obedience than all sacrifices, it should suffice to reject any form of worship that is not approved by the commandment of God.

We have set forth another special part of Christian doctrine: Where should people look for salvation? Furthermore, the knowledge of our salvation has three steps. For it must begin from a sense of our own misery, which should drive us to despair of our souls as if dead. Moreover, that happens when the original, inborn wickedness of our nature is shown to us—the source of all evils. It brings forth in us cowardice, rebellion against God, pride, greed, lust, and every kind of evil desire. Having turned us away from all purity and righteousness, it holds us captive under the true yoke of sin. When their sins are revealed to everyone so that, shamed by their own obscenity, they are forced to be displeased with themselves, they regard all that is their own as nothing. Then, their consciences are summoned to the tribunal of God so that, having acknowledged His curse and accepted the news of eternal death, so to speak, they learn to shudder at the wrath of God. This is the first step on the path to salvation, so that man, humbled and shocked at himself, might despair of every aid of the flesh (yet not harden himself against the judgment of God or become frightened or callous), so that, fearful and anxious, he may groan with pain and long for a remedy. From here he should go up to the second step. That happens when, standing upright, he finds relief in the knowledge of Christ. For nothing else remains for the humbled man for this method that we have articulated except that he turn himself to Christ and be delivered from misery by His benefit. He seeks true salvation in Christ who holds His strength, that is, who acknowledges that He alone is the only priest through whom we are reconciled to the Father, that His death is the one and only sacrifice by which sins were atoned for and the judgment of God was satisfied, having obtained true and perfect righteousness. This person does not divide his righteousness before God between Christ and himself but acknowledges that His benefit is full and free. It is necessary also to climb from this step to the next one, so that he who has been taught about the grace of Christ and the benefit of His death and resurrection may rest in it with strong, solid trust and be certain that he so belongs to Christ that he possesses righteousness and life in Him.

See how miserably this doctrine has been overturned now. Arcane questions about original sin have been addressed in the schools[2] with which they raised this deadly human disease as much as humanly possible. For when they dispute about it, they almost reject the immoderation of gluttony and lust. They offer no word, however, about the blindness and pride of the mind from which unbelief and superstition proceed or about the inner malice of the soul, arrogance, ambition, stubborn disobedience, and other hidden evils. Their sermons are by no means more sound. Now, was the preaching of free will that was being heard before Luther and others came forth capable of nothing else than puffing people up with a proud opinion of their own virtue so that, swollen in their stomach alone, they gave no place to the help and grace of the Holy Spirit? Why would they need as much? There is no greater point of contention among us and in which our enemies more firmly speak against us than justification—whether we obtain it by faith or works. They in no

---

2 Calvin's references to "the schools" refer to the scholastic method of theological investigation, which had been ascendant after the publication of Peter Lombard's *Sentences*. Scholastic theology was focused on making definitions and distinctions, but Calvin thought that it often obscured the teaching of the Bible.

way allow this honor to be attributed to Christ so that He may be called our righteousness, unless the merits of our works also count as a part of it. Here we are not disputing about good works—whether they need to be supplied by the godly, are accepted by God, or have a reward before Him. Rather, we are disputing about whether works reconcile us to God by their own worth; whether we obtain eternal life at their cost; whether they are compensations that are paid to the judgment of God to remove guilt; or whether trust for salvation must be placed in them. Therefore, we rebuke these errors because people are told to regard their own works more than Christ in order to make God favorably disposed to them, merit His grace, obtain the inheritance of eternal life, and finally be righteous before God. First of all, they are proud of the merits of their works, as if they have God bound to them. But what else is this pride than a destructive intoxication of the mind? For they adore themselves in place of Christ, and when they are drowning in the deep whirlpool of death they dream that they have life. But if I seem to exaggerate this point, this troubling doctrine certainly exists in all the schools and churches: that it is necessary to merit the grace of God by works; that eternal life must be obtained by works; that confidence of salvation is rash and presumptuous unless it is propped up by the support of good works; that we are reconciled to God by the satisfaction of good works but not by the free forgiveness of sins; that good works are meritorious for eternal salvation, not because they are freely imputed for righteousness by the merit of Christ but by the terms of the law. There is no free pardon for sins, so they say, but people are reconciled to God as often as they are alienated from His grace by satisfactory works. Help from the merits of Christ and the martyrs is added to satisfactions, yet only in that way does a sinner merit help. It is agreed that the whole world was fascinated with these godless ideas before Luther became known to the world. Moreover, today there is no other part of our doctrine that our enemies attack with more strife and zeal.

Finally, this very deadly error has not only everywhere occupied people's minds but has also been regarded as one of the chief heads of the faith that is not allowed to be doubted: that it is necessary that the faithful continually doubt God's grace toward them and have suspended consciences. But by this diabolical imagination the force of faith was entirely extinguished, the benefit of Christ taken away, and the salvation of the people overturned. For, as Paul testifies, that alone is Christian faith in which trust is stirred in our hearts and in which we dare to stand in the presence of God (Rom. 5:2). It should be pointed out that elsewhere he taught that we have the witness of our adoption sealed within by the Holy Spirit, trusting in Him whom we call God the Father (Rom. 8:15–16).

But what is the point of that hesitation that our enemies require from our disciples except that any faith in the promises of God may vanish? Paul reasons that faith has vanished and the promises have been abolished if the inheritance is from the law (Rom. 4:14). Why is that so? The reason is that the law keeps the person in doubt that he can rest in sure, firm trust. But in opposition to that, those men dream up such a faith that turns a person from the certainty that Paul demands to wishful thinking, so that he bends like a reed. And yet it is not surprising that they fell into such absurdity after they once and for all established faith for salvation in the merits of works. Indeed, it could not have happened otherwise than that they fell into this ruin from that precipice. For what will a person find in his own works except matter for doubting and at last despairing? Therefore, we see that one error dragged another along with it.

O most invincible Caesar and illustrious princes, what I said before must be repeated here for you: the salvation of the church hangs from this doctrine like a man's life does from his soul. If only the purity of its doctrine had been corrupted, the church would already have been wounded with a deadly wound. Therefore, if I show that it was for the most part extinguished, then it will be as if the church were said to have been wounded almost to the point of final ruin. I have indicated that in passing until this point, and I will shed more light on it in a little while. Now I come to those things that I said have resemblance to the body: government and the administration of the sacraments. Even if the external appearance of those things had no evil, the force and use of them had nevertheless died off after the destruction of that doctrine. For there was nothing sane on the inside or the outside, the demonstration of which is easy. In regard to the sacraments, first of all the mysteries instituted by Christ were regarded in the same place as ceremonies invented by humans. Indeed, seven sacraments were received without any distinction. Christ instituted only two of those, while the others were established by human authority alone. These were no less tied to the grace of God than if they had had Christ contained in them. In particular, the two that Christ instituted were corrupted in a dreadful way. Baptism has been wrapped up in so many unnecessary additions that you barely recognize a thin trace of true, pure baptism. The Lord's Supper, however, has not only been corrupted by unnecessary additions but has itself been turned into something entirely different. It is clear what Christ commanded to be done and in what order. But after His command was set aside, a theatrical performance was devised that took the place of the supper. Indeed, how is the Mass similar to the true Lord's Supper? Although, according to the precept of Christ, the faithful should share with each other the holy symbols of the body and blood of the Lord, an excommunication is often seen in the Mass. For the priest separates himself from the rest of the assembled so that he may separately gulp down what should have been held forth and distributed among them. Moreover, as if he were a successor of Aaron, he pretends that he offers a sacrifice to atone for the people's sins. Where did Christ mention sacrifice? He commands us to take, eat, and drink. Who allows people to turn receiving into offering? What is the purpose of that change, except to give up the eternal, inviolable decree of Christ for whimsical human precepts? Certainly, this is a serious evil. But the superstition is far worse still because they apply this work as meritorious to obtain grace for the living and the dead. And so the efficacy of Christ's death was turned into an empty theatrical performance, while at the same time the honor of the Eternal Priest was stolen from Christ that it might be given to people. But when the people are called to communion, they are only admitted to half of it. Why is this? Christ gives the cup to all to drink and commands all to drink from it. Contrary to this, men forbid the assembly of the faithful to touch the cup. In this way, signs that had been joined with an indivisible union by the authority of Christ are separated by the lust of men.

To be sure, the consecration of both baptism and the Mass differs in no way at all from magical incantations. For by breathing and whispering, even in unintelligible words, they think that they bring about mysteries. It is as if Christ wanted His Word to be uttered under one's breath for the performance of the mysteries and not rather declared with a distinct voice. The power, nature, and use of baptism is expressed in the gospel in clear words. In the supper, Christ does not mutter over the bread. Rather, He addresses the Apostles in distinct words when He recites the promise and adds the command that a common confession be proclaimed among the faithful. Now secret exorcisms are inflated in the place of preaching. As I have said, they are more suited for the magical arts than for the sacraments. First, they have already done this wrong: the spectacle of the ceremonies is shown to the people, the meaning and truth of which is kept silent. For there is no other use of the sacraments than when what represents the symbol to the eyes is explained from the Word of God. Therefore, since the people have nothing there but empty forms that feed the eyes, they hear no doctrine that may direct them to the true purpose, and cling closely to the external work itself. Hence that very destructive superstition: they act like the sacraments alone are sufficient for salvation, and caring nothing about repentance, faith, or even Christ Himself, they take the symbols as the reality. And indeed, that wicked dogma—that the sacraments avail by themselves—prevails not only among the uneducated common folk but also in the schools, provided that no one exposes it as mortal sin. It is as if the sacraments were given for another purpose or use than for leading us by the hand to Christ. Add to this the fact that they protect the consecrated bread in a small box in what is more corrupt enchantment than godly ritual, so that it may be adored and invoked in place of Christ. For that reason, if any danger burdens them, they flee together to that bread as if to a single defense. They use it as an amulet against all harm, to seek pardon from God while they make use of the greatest sin. They truly act as if Christ wanted to prostitute His body for improprieties of any sort when He gave it to us in the sacrament. What indeed does the promise contain? It is nothing else than this: as often as we observe His holy supper, we are made sharers of His body and blood. He said, "Take, eat, and drink. This is My body. This is My blood. Do this in remembrance of Me."[3] Do we not see that the promise was included in both elements with their own ends that are necessary to contain themselves within—we who want to seize what is offered there? Therefore, those people are deceived who think that they have something else than common, ordinary bread outside the legitimate use of the supper. But this common defilement of all things was for that reason exposed to the filthy marketplace, as if they had been instituted for no other end than to serve for income. Moreover, the marketplace is not handled secretly or shamefully. Instead, it is exercised in public, no differently than in the merchants' marketplace. It is known that they are for sale, as much as every Mass in every region is. Even their price was established by other people. Finally, if anyone seriously considers the churches, he will see that they do not differ at all from for-profit taverns and that there is no kind of sacred thing that is not for sale there.

If I were to recount the vices of church government, I may find no end of speaking about them. Therefore, I will only briefly make note of some that are very glaring and cannot be hidden. First of all, the pastoral office as it was instituted by Christ is now obsolete. Christ certainly placed bishops and pastors (or by whatever other name they are called) in charge of the church, as Paul testifies, so that they may edify it with sound doctrine. According to this rule, no one is a true pastor of the church except the person who exercises the office of teaching. But today whoever has something close to the title of pastor hands that duty over to others. There is hardly one out of a hundred bishops to be found who ever mounts the lectern to teach. And it is no wonder. For the episcopates have degenerated into offices of governors. But pastors of lower rank, whether they think they fulfill their office in trifles that

---

3 Calvin is paraphrasing here. See Matthew 26:26–28; Mark 22–25; Luke 22:17–20; 1 Corinthians 10:16–21; and 1 Corinthians 11:17–34.

are entirely foreign to the command of Christ or by the example of bishops, toss back this very concern onto the shoulders of others. Hence the
leasings of the priesthood are no less usual than those of estates. What
more do we want? The spiritual government that had been commended
to us by Christ was totally removed from our midst. A new forged kind
of governing was introduced. Although it may be sold under the name
of church government, it nevertheless has no more likeness to it than
the world does to the kingdom of Christ. But if anyone objects that
the fault of those who do not do their duty should not be attributed to
rank, I first respond that the evil rages everywhere, so much that it has
already become public custom. Second, even if we pretend that all bishops and presbyters[4] of lower rank today remain in their own station and
do what they think belongs to their profession, why this instead of what
Christ actually instituted? When they sing or murmur in the temple,
they show off their theatrical clothing and perform many ceremonies.
There is either no concern for teaching, or it is rare. But by the command
of Christ, no one can buy for himself the title of bishop or pastor who
does not feed his flock with the Word of the Lord.

Now, since those who preside over the church should excel and shine
beyond others by the example of a very holy life, how well are those fit
for their calling in this respect who hold this position today? Although
the world has come to the highest point of corruption, there is nevertheless no order more packed full of every kind of shameful action. Would
that their own innocence may disprove what I am saying. How readily
would I retract it. But their obscenity was exposed before the eyes of all.
Their unexplainable avarice and greed lies open, as does their intolerable
arrogance and cruelty. By received custom and practice, they fill their
houses with the loud noise of their impure dances, burn with zeal for
dice games, and are controlled by gluttonous eating habits. They boast
of delicacies and every kind of luxury as outstanding virtues. As I pass

---

4   "Bishop" translates the Greek word *episkopos* (i.e., "overseer"), while "presbyter" or
    "priest" translates the Greek word *presbyteros* (i.e., "elder"). Protestants see these as differ-
    ent descriptions of one office, while the Roman Catholic Church sees them as separate
    offices.

over other matters, how much corruption does celibacy have, in which the elite want to be regarded as single? It makes me ashamed to disclose those secrets that I prefer to be corrected in a silent manner. And so I will not mention any hidden vices, for more than enough filth and corruption is now otherwise apparent. How rarely, I ask, is a priest free from prostitution? How many houses are infamous for daily debauchery? How many pure families are defiled by their raging lusts? To be sure, I take no pleasure in elaborating their vices; nor is it my plan to do so. It is worthwhile, nevertheless, to consider how much those vices, which today are visible everywhere in the priestly order, differ from what is required of true ministers of Christ and the church.

It is also not the least significant part of church government to choose and appoint those who will rule in a right and orderly manner. We have the rule for which it is necessary to conduct all elections from the Word of God. Many decrees of ancient councils exist that wisely and carefully prescribe everything that relates to the proper form of electing them. If our enemies could put forth even one example of a canonical election, I would concede that they have succeeded. We know what sort of examination the Holy Spirit requires of a pastor through the mouth of Paul (in his letters to Timothy and Titus), which the ancient sanctions of the fathers also required. Today when people are made bishops, is there really consideration of any such thing? No, how rarely are there any of them who are raised to this rank endowed at least moderately with those talents without which there could not be suitable ministers of the church? We see that the Apostles maintained this order when they put ministers in charge, which the ancient church then followed, and which the ancient canons required to be observed. If I complain that this is ignored and rejected today, will it not be a fair complaint? What shall I say if, after every virtue is trampled on, vice is promoted with the basest shamelessness? But this is unknown to no one. For ecclesiastical honors are either bought at a price that is agreed on, occupied by force and fist, procured by evil bargains, or obtained by corrupted allegiances. Sometimes there are rewards even for pimping and such arts. Finally, church honors are much more shamelessly pursued than any profane possessions ever.

And would that the government of the church were corrupted in such a way that those who rule only sinned against themselves or at least did not harm others except by bad example. But this evil supersedes all the rest—that they exercise very cruel tyranny and indeed over souls. No indeed, what else is the authority of the church that is thrown around today than licentious power over souls, without law and order, which oppresses them with a very miserable bondage? Christ permitted the sort of authority to the Apostles that God had conferred on the prophets earlier and that included certain ends, particularly that they would exercise the office of ambassador for themselves in the midst of the people. Furthermore, this law of the office of ambassador is perpetual, so that the person who is sent may faithfully and wholeheartedly fulfill the commands that he has received. This is also expressly articulated by the Apostles: "Go, teach all the nations what I have taught you" (Matt. 28:19; Mark 16:15). Likewise, the Apostles required that nothing else be preached than the gospel. If one inquires about the authority with which successors have been endowed, Peter defines it when he commands all who speak in the church to speak God's words (1 Peter 4:11). But now those who want to be regarded as rulers of the church wrongfully seize this license for themselves—to say whatever they want. As soon as they have spoken, they are heard without any examination. They will object that this is a false accusation. For they lay hold of no other law for themselves than that they determine by their own authority what the Holy Spirit has revealed. Therefore, they will deny that they subject the consciences of the faithful to their own advice or their own lust; instead, they will say that they promote only the oracles of the Spirit that have been revealed to them and have the added confirmation of others. This is an ingenious pretext indeed. No one doubts that those things must be obeyed without delay which they have received from the Holy Spirit and teach. But when they submit that they can teach nothing else than the mere oracles of the Holy Spirit because they are guided by Him, it is not possible that whatever they establish is true because they sit on the thrones of truth. Do they not thereby measure their authority by lust? For if any of their decrees should be held as oracles in which there is no exception, their power is unlimited. Which tyrant ever has so abused the patience of his subjects that whatever he decided he would command a decree to be received as if it were from heaven? Certainly, tyrants want their edicts of every sort to be obeyed. But those men demand far more—that we believe that the Holy Spirit speaks when they force on us what they have dreamed up.

And so, we see how they, armed with this authority, have held the souls of the faithful bound fast to a harsh, unjust bondage. More laws were established on top of other ones, which provided very many snares for consciences. For they applied them not to external order but to the spiritual government even over the inner soul. And there was no end until that immense multitude came about, which is no different than a labyrinth. And some laws appear to have been made entirely to torture and harass consciences. Furthermore, their observance is severely avenged, as if the whole force of godliness consisted in them. Although, when the commands of God have been broken, either no question is raised or light penalties are applied; anything done contrary to human decrees is nevertheless regarded as very heinous sin. Because the church is oppressed by this tyrannical yoke, if anyone dares to speak a contrary word, he is immediately condemned as a heretic. Finally, to let out a free sigh is a capital offense. And so that they may preserve this possession of unbearable domination, they prevent the people from reading and understanding Holy Scripture with bloodthirsty edicts. They hurl darts of fire at those who stir up controversy about their authority, so that they allow almost no inquiry about religion now.

When the truth was suffocated by such pervasive, thick darkness; when religion was polluted by so many godless superstitions; when the worship of God was corrupted by horrid sacrilege and His glory was lying prostrate; when the benefit of redemption was buried under many twisted opinions, people drunk on the destructive confidence of works sought salvation elsewhere than in Christ, the administration of the sacraments was partly mangled and destroyed, partly corrupted by many human inventions mixed in, partly defiled by for-profit markets; when the government of the church had degenerated into a totally confused wasteland; when those who were sitting in the place of pastors first damaged the church very much by a loose way of living; when they exercised harsh and especially harmful tyranny over souls, the people were led like a herd of cattle to destruction by every kind of error— Luther emerged, then others appeared, who with united devotion sought out reasons and ways by which religion could be freshly purged from so many corruptions, the doctrine of godliness be restored to its purity, and the church be brought together out of such distress into a tolerable condition. We still proceed in this course today.

And because I said in advance that I would speak about the remedies that we applied for the correction of those evils, I will describe not so much the manner in which we proceeded (for this will appear later) but rather, as it is apparent, that our efforts have had nothing else in view than that the condition of the church might become better than that worst one, at least to some degree. Our doctrine has been attacked and is daily attacked by many arrogant false accusations of many people. Some bravely preach against it in sermons. Others abuse and degrade it in published books. Very many things are brought together by both, by which they believe it can be defamed among the ignorant. But the confession of our faith that we offered to your majesty, O most invincible Caesar, still exists in the hands of men. It reflects for us a glowing testimony of how undeservedly we are harassed by so much hateful slander. And so far we have always been prepared to give an account of our doctrine, as we also do today. In short, no doctrine is heard in our churches besides what we publicly profess. Controversial topics are explained clearly and with good faith in the confession, and no part of them is not extensively addressed and carefully explained by our men. From this, one can establish from just judgment how far removed we are from all ungodliness. Surely this is agreed upon by the just and unjust: our people have benefited the church in no small way. For they stirred up the world as if from the dark depths of ignorance to the reading of Scripture, greatly devoted themselves to a purer understanding of it, and readily made clear certain topics of Christian doctrine that are especially useful to know. As for our enemies, hardly anything was heard in their sermons besides old wives' tales or comments no less irrelevant. Schools were roaring with debates over questions, but Scripture was rarely mentioned there. Those who were holding the power of government had this one concern: that no profit would be missed. Therefore, they endured whatever was for meals without difficulty. Certainly even the most unjust people concede that our men brought some change to these evils, however much they later defamed our doctrine with many false accusations.

But I would not want this to prevail to lighten blame, if we have harmed anything in any way: that the church has greatly benefited from our labors. Therefore, let our whole doctrine, custom of administering the sacraments, and method of governing the church be examined. In these three matters we will not be found to have changed from that ancient form anything that we did not try to restore to the right norm of God's Word. And to return to that distinction put forth by us earlier, all those controversial matters between us concerning doctrine pertain either to the lawful worship of God or to the firm assurance of our salvation. Certainly we exhort people to worship God neither coldly nor negligently, and in defining the manner we neither depart from its purpose nor omit anything that applies to the matter. We preach the glory of God far more magnificently than it used to be preached before us. We labor sincerely so that the virtues in which it shines may become more and more known. We exalt His benefits toward us with as many praises as possible. Hence people are stirred up to revere His majesty, to display to Him the reverence worthy of His greatness, to be truly grateful from the heart, and to confess His praises. Hence firm confidence in Him is brought forth in their hearts, which later produces invocation. Hence also everyone is prepared for the true denial of self so that, as the will is disposed to the obedience of God, one may bid farewell to one's own desires. Finally, as God wants to be worshiped by us in a spiritual manner, so we with wholehearted devotion insist on urging all sacrifices of the Spirit that He commends to us.

Indeed, not even our enemies can deny that we are diligent in these admonitions. Moreover, people do not desire any goods from elsewhere than what they expect from God. They confide in His power. They take comfort in His goodness. They rely on His truth. They are brought to

Him with all the affection of the heart. They lean on Him full of hope. They need Him in necessity, that is, every moment. They bring all goods that they have received to Him, and they confirm that with a confession of praise. And lest they be scared by a difficult approach, we have shown that the fountain of all goods has been set forth to us in Christ, from which we drink whatever is necessary for us. Our books and sermons are witnesses that we frequently and zealously commend true repentance, so that people may renounce the way and the desires of their flesh and themselves entirely, by which, disposed to obedience to the one God, they may live no longer for themselves but for Him. Moreover, we do not omit the outward duties and works of love that follow such a renewal. To be sure, this is a certain and by no means false way of worshiping God, which we know He approves of, just as He has commanded in His Word. These are the only sacrifices of the Christian church, which have God as witness.

Therefore, since one God is adored in our churches with pure rite and without any superstition; since His goodness, wisdom, power, truth, and other virtues are preached more abundantly than in any other place ever; since He is invoked with true faith in the name of Christ; since people extol His benefits with their hearts and tongues; since they are constantly called back to simple and sincere obedience to Him; finally, since nothing is heard there that does not have a view to promoting the hallowing of His name; what reason is there that they so badly receive us who profess ourselves Christians? First, as it is necessary, we sharply rebuke such crass idolatries that are sought after everywhere in the world, which those who prefer darkness to light cannot endure. While God is adored in images, humanly devised forms of worship are instituted in His name; while God is entreated for the images of saints, divine honors are displayed in the bones of the dead, et cetera—abominations—we call them what they are. For this reason, those who regard our doctrine hatefully inveigh against us. They make us out to be heretics—we who dare to overthrow the worship of God currently approved of by the church. They repeatedly toss around that term *church* in the place of a shield, which we will see a little later. Meanwhile, what is that stubbornness, in which such shameful corruptions of the worship of God are apparent, that not only keeps them but also conceals them, besides arrogantly burying the very worship of God?

Both sides confess that idolatry is a damnable evil before God. When we attack the worship of images, our enemies immediately oppose us so that they may adapt their patronage to the evil that they had condemned together with us in word. To be sure, what is more ridiculous is that, although they agree with us about the Greek word, when it is translated into Latin, they first begin to oppose us. Indeed, they boldly defend the veneration of images, even though they condemn idolatry. But clever people deny that the honor of worship (*latria*), which they display with their images, exists. But if they are compared to the ancient idolaters, a likeness, as it were, is present among them. They put forward the pretext that they worship heavenly gods but under bodily figures that represent them. What other pretexts do those men put forth? Is it really true that God allows Himself to be satisfied with such excuses? Did the prophets really cease to rebuke the madness of the Egyptians because they brought forth subtleties from the arcane mysteries of their theology, with which they got off? Do we also think that the bronze serpent was adored in the same way by the Jews—only because it was regarded as honor for the image of God? "The gentiles," says Ambrose, "adore wood because they think it is the image of God."[5] But the invisible image of God exists not in what is seen but in what is certainly not seen. But what is being done today? Do they not prostrate themselves before images as if they had God present there? Furthermore, do they tie the power and grace of God to anything besides statues and pictures, or flee to them when they want to pray?

And the more crass superstitions have not yet been mentioned. These cannot be attributed to uneducated people because they are approved by public consent. They decorate their idols with flowers and crowns, robes, clothes, belts, moneybags, and every kind of inappropriate thing. They

---

5   See Ambrose in *Psal. 118*. Ambrose (c. 339–97) was archbishop of Milan from 374 until his death. He was an influential church leader and opponent of Arianism.

approach them with candles, burn sacrifices of incense, and carry them on their shoulders in the procession. They flock together from distant regions to one statue, even though they have similar ones at home. Similarly, although there are more images in one church—whether of Mary or someone else—than in previous times, one is frequented as if it were more divine. When they pray to the image of Christopher or Barbara, they sing to them the Lord's Prayer with the angelic greeting. The more beautiful or smoky the images, the more prestige they attribute to them. New support is also added by tales of miracles. They fabricate that some have spoken oracles from God, others have restrained fires at the foot of the church, others have emigrated of their own will to a new dwelling place, and others have fallen down from heaven. Although the whole world teems with these and similar follies and it lies open before all, we, nevertheless, who restored and diligently serve to restore the worship of the one God to the norm of His Word, we who are pure and have purified our churches from every form of idolatry and superstition, are accused of violating the worship of God because we removed the veneration of images, that is, idolatry, as we indeed translate, but *idolodulia*, as our enemies prefer.

But besides such clear testimony of Scripture, which they often contradict, the authority of the ancient church also supports us. For as many writers of a purer age are still extant, they describe the abuse of images among the gentiles no differently than what is often seen in the world today, and whatever is said by them applies just as much to our age as to the very people whom they were rebuking at that time. Moreover, there is an easy response to the charge that they level against us for removing images as well as the bones and relics of the saints. For all these things should not be more highly regarded than the bronze serpent, and there was no less reason for these to be removed than for the bronze serpent to be broken to pieces by Hezekiah. It is certain that the *idolomania*, as the minds of men are now enthralled with it, can be cured in no other way than by removing the matter that is causing the madness. And our experience has more than sufficiently proven that the following comment of Augustine is most true: "While looking at an image, no one prays or adores who is not so moved that he thinks he is heard by it."[6] Likewise, images avail more to bend the unhappy soul than to straighten it, because they have mouths, eyes, ears, and feet, but they do not speak, see, hear, or walk. Likewise, this is done while the shapes of their members are dislocated in a certain manner: a soul living in a body decides to think that the body that it sees is most similar to its own. But regarding relics, it is unbelievable to say how foolishly the world has been deceived. I can mention three foreskins of Christ, fourteen nails that are put on display for those three with which He was nailed to the cross, three tunics for that seamless one for which soldiers cast lots, two inscriptions that were posted to the cross, three spears by which Christ's side was pierced, and about five sets of linen clothes with which His body was wrapped in the tomb. In addition, all the utensils of the Holy Supper are displayed, as are an infinite number of inappropriate things of this sort. There is no saint or somewhat famous person to whom they have not attributed two or three bodies. I can name the place where a pumice stone was regarded with great honor as the famous Peter. And I am prevented by shame to mention other filthier things. Therefore, we are wrongly accused because we devoted ourselves to purge the church of God from such corruptions.

Next, in regard to the worship of God, our enemies accuse us because, having omitted what is empty, inappropriate, and disposed only to hypocrisy, we worship God more simply. For reality testifies that nothing was diminished by us in the spiritual worship of God. Rather, since it was for the most part obsolete, we restored it anew. Now let us see whether they are rightfully enraged at us. In regard to doctrine, I say here that we have a common cause with the prophets. For, regarding idolatry, there is nothing that they attack more sharply in their people than placing the worship of God in external splendor with false belief. But what do the prophets proclaim in sum? They say that God neither cares for nor regards ceremonies to be of value if they are esteemed only

---

6   See Augustine, *Epist. 49 et in Psalm 113.* Augustine (354–430) was bishop of Hippo Regius in North Africa from 395 until his death, a theologian, and an apologist. He is perhaps the most influential Christian theologian after the Apostle Paul.

in themselves. They say that God looks at the faith and truth of the heart. Moreover, they say that God neither commanded nor approves of ceremonies with another end than that they may belong to faith, pure invocation, and the exercise of praise. The writings of all the prophets are full of attestations to this. And as I have said, there was no other matter in which they labored more. To be sure, it cannot be denied without foolishness that the world was seized by this blindness more than ever when our men stepped forward. Therefore, it was necessary to urge people with these prophetic rebukes and to drag them away forcefully as it were from that madness, in order that they might no longer believe that God is satisfied with mere ceremonies like childish theatrical shows. Similarly, that doctrine concerning the spiritual worship of God, which had vanished from the memory of the people, had to be urged. Our books and sermons bear clear witness that we have done both of these things until now and still do them.

But because we have inveighed against the ceremonies themselves and have also in some places abolished a great deal of them, in this matter we confess that we share a fair amount in common with the prophets. For they certainly inveighed against their people because they were obstructing the worship of God in external ceremonies, but ones that had been instituted by God Himself. We complain that the same honor is held for humanly devised inappropriate things. Those men, having condemned superstitions, left intact a multitude of ceremonies that God had enjoined and that were useful and fitting for the pedagogical age. We took care to correct the many rites that they had rashly crawled to or had turned into abuse, because they by no means agree with the time. For, unless we want to confuse everything, the distinction between the Old Testament and the New Testament must always be maintained. For ceremonies, the useful observance of which existed under the law, are now not only superfluous but absurd and evil. For when Christ was absent and not yet revealed, they nourished the souls of the faithful by foreshadowing the hope of His advent, but now they obscure nothing other than His present, conspicuous glory. We see what God did. For He abolished forever those ceremonies that He Himself had commanded for a time. We hear the reason from the mouth of Paul: first, after the body was revealed in Christ, the shadows should have departed; second, God wants to teach the church now in no other way (Gal. 4:3ff; Col. 2:4, 14, 17). Since God set His church free from the bondage that He had imposed on it, what is that evil that allows the people to raise up a new one in place of the old one? Since God has instituted a certain economy, how arrogant is it to establish one that is openly contrary to it and rejected by Him? But it is very evil that, since God has so frequently prohibited all humanly devised worship with severe sanctions, He was being worshiped only by human fabrications. Therefore, why is it that our enemy cries out that religion has been destroyed by us in this matter? First, we have attacked nothing at all except what Christ regards as nothing, since He declares that God is worshiped in vain by human traditions. But perhaps it might have been tolerable in some way if people, by worshiping God in a useless way, destroyed the work. But since elsewhere, in many places, as I said, He forbids new forms of worship to be established for Him beyond His Word, confirms that He is seriously offended by this audacity, and threatens no light penalty, it is agreed that the correction we have applied was forced by great necessity.

But it does not escape my notice how difficult it is to persuade the world of this: God rejects and even hates whatever is devised by human reason for His worship. There are several reasons for this error. Everyone thinks his own is excellent, as the ancient proverb says, for which reason it happens that what is born in our own head pleases us more. Moreover, those fabricated forms of worship are often disposed to a certain appearance of wisdom, as Paul also confesses (Col. 2:23). Furthermore, since they have very much external splendor that falls before the eyes, they smile at us more—at our fleshly nature—than those things alone that God requires and approves, since the latter are less ostentatious. Yet nothing darkens the minds of men more, so that they make a wrong judgment about this matter, than hypocrisy. For although it is necessary for true worshipers of God to bring forth heart and soul, people always want to invent a manner of serving God that is entirely different from that, so that rendering service of the body to Him, they keep their soul for themselves. Furthermore, while they thrust upon Him external pomp, they think that by this cunning they have escaped from the duty to offer themselves to Him. And this is the reason that people very readily undertake countless acts of worship in which they are miserably worn out without purpose or measure, and that they prefer to wander continuously in a labyrinth than to worship God simply in Spirit and in truth.

Therefore, it is false accusation that our enemies accuse us of attracting people with ease and complaisance. For if the option should be given, the fleshly man would always choose anything instead of agreeing to worship God according to the mandates of our doctrine. It is easy to mention faith and repentance, but the things are very difficult to produce. Therefore, whoever establishes that the worship of God consists in these things least eases the reins on people; instead, he forces order on it, at which they especially dread to arrive. We have very rich testimony of this in the matter itself. People allow themselves to be bound by very many harsh laws, to be reduced to very many laborious observances, to have imposed upon them a rigid, heavy yoke, and to have any kind of harm done to them, provided that the heart is not mentioned. Hence it is apparent that nothing more escapes the natural character of man than that spiritual truth about which we diligently preach. For it is buried in that splendor on which our enemy so greatly insists. The very majesty of God forces out the fact that we cannot banish ourselves from His worship. Therefore, while we cannot avoid the necessity of worshiping God, we seek out diversions on the side, so that it may not be necessary to come right into His presence. Or instead, with external ceremonies as beautiful masks, we hide the inner malice of the heart and prop up services of the body as an intermediary wall, lest we be forced to approach Him with the heart. With utmost regret does the world allow such deceits to be shaken from them, and hence those tears exist because they were dragged by us into the open light out of those dark secrets with which they were securely playing with God.

In regard to prayer, we have corrected three things. For, having bid farewell to the intercession of the saints, we have called people back to

Christ, so that they may invoke the Father in His name and learn to rely on Him as mediator. Moreover, we have taught them to pray first with solid and firm confidence and second with understanding. For before, they were muttering over confused prayers in an unknown language. Here we are defamed with cruel insults—first, that we are insulting the saints, and second, that we are depriving the faithful of a huge benefit. But we deny both charges. For our not allowing the office of Christ to be attributed to the saints is done without harm to any of them. Therefore, we do not prematurely take away any honor from them but only what was rashly and wrongfully attributed to them by human error. I will say nothing that cannot be pointed to with the finger. First of all, people about to pray imagine that God is far away and that there is no access to Him except by the leadership of some patron. Moreover, this false opinion does not wander about only among uncultured and uneducated folk, but those who want to be regarded as leaders of the blind are also thus persuaded. Furthermore, in seeking out patrons, everyone follows his own purpose. One person chooses Mary, another Michael, and another Peter. For the most part, they give Christ no place or number among them. No indeed, scarcely one in a hundred is found who is not shocked as if at a new omen, if he hears Christ named as advocate. Therefore, having passed over Christ, everyone is satisfied with the patronage of the saints. Next, superstition swells more and more, so that they indiscriminately invoke the saints—no differently than God. I do indeed admit that when they want to speak more distinctly, they seek nothing else from the saints than that their prayers be assisted before God. But most often, having confounded this distinction, they beg and plead to God sometimes and to the saints at other times—wherever the impulse of the mind brings them. Moreover, each one is assigned its own sphere, so that one brings forth rain, another good weather, another delivers from fever, and another from shipwreck. But so that I may conceal those corrupt follies of the gentiles that are nevertheless prevalent everywhere in the churches, let this one act of wickedness suffice for all: the whole world, by summoning advocates from here and there, neglects Christ who alone was set forth by God and trusts more in the protection of the saints than in the protection of God.

But our detractors, even those who among others have a good deal more equity, desire a measure in us because we have entirely removed the mention of dead saints from prayers. But I would like them to tell me why they think those sin who faithfully observe the rule laid down by Christ (the best teacher) and all the prophets and Apostles, and who do not omit anything that the Holy Spirit has taught in Scripture or the servants of God have held in use from the origin of the world until the age of the Apostles. There is hardly anything else about which the Holy Spirit very carefully commands than the true method of prayer. There is no syllable that teaches us to flee to the aid of dead saints. Many prayers of very many of the faithful exist. In them there is not even one example of such a practice. Sometimes the Israelites did indeed ask God to remember Abraham, Isaac, and Jacob, and David likewise. But they meant nothing else by those words but that, mindful of His covenant that He had made with them, He might bless their posterity according to His promise. For the covenant of grace, which was ratified at last in Christ, those holy fathers had received in their own name and in that of their posterity. Therefore, by such mention of the fathers, the faithful of the Israelite church do not seek support from the dead but simply appeal to the promise that was entrusted to them until, ratified in the hand of Christ, it would be fulfilled. Therefore, how insane is the curiosity, the form of prayer that the Lord commended to us having been abandoned, that introduces the intercession of the saints into our prayers without any doctrine or example? But so that I may briefly conclude this point, I follow in the footsteps of the teaching of Paul that there is no true invocation of God except what is born from faith and that faith is born from the Word of God (Rom. 10:14). Unless I am mistaken, he sufficiently expressed in those words that there is no other firm foundation of prayer than the Word of God. And since elsewhere he commands that faith, that is, assurance of conscience, must precede every activity of life, he shows that it is required especially in this, even more than in everything else. Yet this is even more applicable to our present cause: he testifies that prayer depends on the Word of God. Indeed, it is as if He prohibits all people from opening their mouths unless God precedes the words. This is a bronze wall for us, which all the gates of hell will try in vain to demolish. Therefore, since a clear command exists about invoking the one God; since one mediator is set forth by whose intercession our prayers should be propped up; since the promise is also added that whatever we seek in the name of Christ we will obtain; people will pardon us if we follow the sure truth of God rather than their worthless inventions.

Surely it is necessary for those who hold the intercession of the dead before God in their prayers so that, helped by it, they may more easily obtain what they seek to prove one of two things: (1) that they were thus taught by the Word of God, or (2) that it is lawful for people to pray however they want. But it is clear that those principles were not established by any testimony of Scripture or proven example of the saints. But in regard to the second matter, Paul loudly contradicts it, because he denies that God can be invoked except by those who have been instructed to pray by His Word. Hence it is fitting that prayer depends on faith, with which godly minds must be equipped and instructed when they draw near to pray. The world makes supplication to God, while being doubtful about its success. For they do not lean on the promise or perceive the value of having a mediator through whom they will certainly obtain what they ask for. Furthermore, God commands us to come without any hesitation at all (Matt. 21:22). Thus, prayer that proceeds from true faith procures God's grace, whereas the same, united with hesitation, alienates Him from us instead. Indeed, this is the peculiar mark that distinguishes the pure invocation of the one God from the profane, wandering prayers of the gentiles. Consequently, when true faith is taken away, prayer ceases to be the worship of God. And that is what James meant: "Let the person who lacks wisdom ask for it from God. But let him ask in faith without hesitating. For the person who hesitates is like a wave of the sea that is driven and seized by the force of the wind" (James 1:6). But it is no wonder if, having abandoned Christ the true mediator, they thus waver in uncertainty and timidity. For He is the one, as Paul says, through whom we have boldness and access to the Father with confidence (Rom. 5:2; Eph. 2:18). Therefore, we have taught people to be brought to Christ by praying no longer with hesitation or wavering, as they used to do. We have commanded them to rest in the secure Word of the Lord instead, because once it penetrates the soul, it casts far away every doubt that opposes faith.

There remains the third vice that I said that we had corrected in regard to prayer. Since people were generally praying in an unknown language, we taught them to pray with understanding. Therefore, according to our doctrine everyone is instructed to pray privately, so that they understand what they are asking of God. The public prayers in our churches were also composed in such a way that they could be understood by everyone. Natural reason also dictates this, even if God had commanded nothing about it. This indeed is the purpose of prayer: that people may make God aware of and a witness to their necessities and pour out their hearts before Him, as it were. Therefore, nothing is more foreign to this than to move the tongue without the mind or understanding. But such foolishness came about that it was nearly considered sacrilegious to pray in a vernacular language. I can name one archbishop who threatened imprisonment and harsher penalties on anyone who prays the Lord's Prayer in a language other than Latin. Otherwise, this was generally the persuasion of all people: nothing forbids anyone to pray in their own language at home, provided that the ultimate intention of the mind, as they say, is determined to pray. But this mostly seemed to prevail in churches: that solemn prayers should not be expressed in any other language than Latin.

Certainly, as I just said, there is the similar monstrosity of wanting to have a conversation with God with an empty sound of the tongue. Even if God Himself did not testify that it displeases Him, nature itself (without any adviser) rejects it. Besides, it is clear from the whole doctrine of Scripture how much God detests such fabrication. Moreover, the words of Paul about the public prayers of the church are clear: ignorant people cannot respond "amen" if a blessing is made in a foreign language (1 Cor. 14:16). It is therefore more astonishing that they have increased their shamelessness who first introduced this very corrupt custom, so that they pursue this very thing, as if it were suitable for the majesty of prayer, which Paul regards as utterly absurd. Therefore, let our enemies mock our method as much as they want—that all the people in our churches pray together to God in the popular language, and men and women without distinction sing the Psalms—provided that the Holy Spirit bears witness for us from heaven that He rejects the confused voices that are offered elsewhere without true spirit.

In the second special part of doctrine, which addresses where human salvation is situated and the way by which people can arrive at it, many questions are contained. For, since we command people to seek righteousness and life outside of themselves, that is, in Christ alone, because within themselves they have nothing but sin and death, first a controversy arises among us about free will and its abilities. And indeed, if a person succeeds in meriting anything by himself before God, he no longer seeks salvation altogether in the grace of Christ but attributes part of it to himself. On the other hand, if a person's entire salvation that he has received is attributed to the grace of Christ, there is nothing left for the person to do by which he may help himself, namely to obtain salvation by his own strength. But our enemies concede that a person is helped to do good by the Holy Spirit in such a way that they nevertheless claim a part for the person. They do this because they do not understand how great of a wound was inflicted on our nature by the fall of the first man. To be sure, they confess original sin together with us. But later they minimize its power when they claim that human abilities were only weakened but not totally depraved. And so they determine that man, infected by the original corruption, is certainly not sufficiently equipped to do good because of the weakness of his abilities; yet helped by the grace of God, he also has something of his own that he confers by himself. But, although we do not deny that man acts voluntarily and with free will when he is guided by the Holy Spirit, we nevertheless assert that his whole nature was permeated with that depravity, with the result that it is absolutely useless to do good by himself. Therefore, on that point we only differ from those who oppose our doctrine because they neither sufficiently humble man nor extol the benefit of regeneration for its worth. We, however, so prostrate man that, reduced to nothing in regard to spiritual righteousness, he learns to seek from God not part of righteousness but the whole of it. Perhaps we do seem to some people who are unjust judges to exceed measure. But our doctrine is neither absurd nor contrary to Holy Scripture or the consensus of the ancient church. Rather, it is possible to confirm whatever we have taught on every issue, even to the letter, from the mouth of Augustine. Therefore, several of those who are otherwise unfavorably disposed toward our cause, because they have a bit more sound judgment, do not dare to contradict us on this point. Certainly we do not differ from the others, as I have said, except that we better equip man, convinced of his own need and powerlessness, for true humility so that, having wholly abandoned trust in himself, he may lean entirely on God. We also better equip man for gratitude, so that whatever good he has he assigns to the kindness of God, just as it is in fact from Him. But they, drunk on a twisted opinion of their own strength, fall headlong to destruction, and they are puffed up with wicked arrogance toward God, lest they attribute the glory of righteousness less to themselves than to God. A third evil is also added: their academic discussions on the corruption of the whole human nature generally stay fixed on the more crass lusts of the flesh, but they do not touch the inner diseases that are far deadlier. In this way it happens that those who are taught in their school about the most hideous sins securely ignore their own, provided they are hidden, as if they themselves do not sin.

The next question that follows concerns the merit and worth of works. To be sure, we honor good works with genuine praise, and we do not deny that reward has been reserved for them before God. But we do take three exceptions on which the whole hinge of the dispute that still remains concerning human salvation turns. First, we say that whatever works may belong to any person, he is nevertheless regarded as righteous before God from nothing else than free mercy, because God, without any regard to works, freely embraces him in Christ by imputing the righteousness of Christ to him as if it were his own. We call this the righteousness of faith, that is, when a person, free from and empty of any trust in works, decides for himself that this alone is the method by which he is accepted by God: he obtains from Christ the righteousness that he lacks. The world is always deluded on this point (for this error has raged in nearly every age), imagining that a person, however imperfect he may be in part, nevertheless merits a certain amount of favor before God by works. But Scripture declares that everyone is cursed who does not fully observe everything that was written in the book of the law. It is necessary to subject to this curse everyone who is esteemed by works. Moreover, no one is delivered from that curse except the person who, having bid farewell entirely to trust in works, puts on Christ, so that he is regarded as righteous in Him by the free acceptance of God. Therefore, we are righteous because God reconciles us to Himself not in view of any works of our own but only Christ's, and by free adoption He makes us His children who were children of wrath. Indeed, as long as God regards our own works, He finds no reason why He should love us. Therefore, it is necessary that, having buried our sins, He bring to us Christ's obedience that He has accepted and embrace us as righteous by His merit. This is the clear and enduring doctrine of Scripture, which certainly has testimony, as Paul says, from the Law and Prophets (Rom. 3:21), but by the gospel it is made so plain that no brighter light should be desired. Paul compares the righteousness of the law with the righteousness of the gospel, locating the former in works and the latter in the grace of Christ (Rom. 10:5, etc.). And he does not divide our being regarded as righteous before God between works and Christ but attributes it entirely to Christ.

At this juncture, two questions arise: (1) whether the glory of our salvation may be divided between us and God, and (2) whether our consciences can securely find rest in God's presence by confidence in works. Paul answers the first question in this way: "That every mouth may be stopped and the whole world may be held accountable by God" . . . "all are equally guilty of unrighteousness and lack glory, but are freely justified by His grace through the redemption that is in Christ Jesus, and that was a display of His righteousness, so that He may be just and the one who justifies Him who has faith in Christ" (Rom. 3:19, 23, etc.). Hence, he concludes that any boasting of the flesh is excluded. We simply follow this explanation. Our enemies, however, contradict us, claiming no differently that a person is justified by the grace of God, but that part of the praise resides in his own works. Concerning the second question, Paul reasons in this way: if the inheritance were by the law, faith would be useless and the promise would be reduced to nothing. From this he concludes that we obtain the inheritance by faith, so that the promise may be firm (Rom. 4:14ff). Likewise, people who have been justified have peace in Christ and no longer fear the presence of God (Rom. 5:1). But he understands that (which every one of us experiences for ourselves) it cannot happen otherwise than that we are plagued by constant restlessness and our consciences waver, as long as they look to the protection of works. Moreover, we only enjoy peaceful and calm serenity when we have given ourselves to Christ as to the only gateway to true confidence. We add nothing to this doctrine. But what Paul considers a massive absurdity—that our consciences be troubled with doubt—our enemies regard as among the first principles of their faith.

The second exception that we take relates to the forgiveness of sins. For certainly our enemies, since they cannot deny that people fall short during their entire lives and often even fall, are also forced to confess that all people need forgiveness through which the defect of righteousness is filled. But later they devise satisfactions with which those who have sinned pay for God's favor. In this place they put contrition first, then works of supererogation (as they call them),[7] and finally punishments that are inflicted on sinners by God. Next, because they understand that those compensations are still far from the righteous measure, they introduce a new kind of satisfaction from elsewhere, namely from the benefit of the keys. More specifically, they say that the treasury of the church is unlocked with the keys, so that what is lacking in us may be filled by the merits of Christ and the saints.[8] We, however, assert that people's sins are freely

---

7   Works of supererogation are works that accrue more merit than the one who does them needs to get into heaven.

8   The extra merit of works of supererogation is deposited in the treasury of merit, where they can be acquired by ordinary Roman Catholics through various means, including pilgrimages, works of devotion, or the purchase of indulgences.

forgiven, and we acknowledge no other satisfaction than what Christ performed when He made atonement for our sins by the sacrifice of His death. Therefore, we declare that forgiveness comes from the benefit of Christ alone, so that we are reconciled to God. Moreover, no compensations come into account here, because our heavenly Father, content with the atonement of Christ alone, requires none from us. We have very clear proof of this doctrine of ours from Scripture, and yet it must not be called ours but rather that of the universal church. For the Apostle sets forth the only way of returning to favor with God: "He who knew no sin became sin for us, so that we might become the righteousness of God in Him" (2 Cor. 5:21). And elsewhere, when he is speaking about the forgiveness of sins, he testifies that righteousness is imputed to us by it, apart from works (Rom. 4:5). Therefore, it is a damnable blasphemy that our enemies dream up that by their satisfactions they merit reconciliation with God and pay for penalties required by His judgment. We assert this firmly just as it is. For in this way what Isaiah taught about Christ is destroyed: "He endured the chastisement of our peace" (Isa. 53:5). There are many reasons that we also reject that foolish fiction regarding works of supererogation, but two are especially severe: (1) it is in no way tolerable that a person can offer to God more than he should, and for the most part they nominally understand the voluntary worship which, when people impose on God things invented by their own brains, they lose time and trouble; and (2) it is far from the case that they should be regarded as expiations for placating the wrath of God. Furthermore, we neither should have endured nor did in fact endure mixing the blood of Christ with the blood of martyrs in such a way that it becomes an indiscriminate pile of merits or satisfactions to pay for the penalties that are required for sins. "For the blood of no martyr," as Augustine said, "was shed for the forgiveness of sins."[9] That was the work of Christ alone, in which He has brought us together not to imitate it but to rejoice in it. Leo very clearly agrees with this when he writes the following: "However precious the death of many saints has been in the sight of God, the killing of no innocent person,

---

9 See Augustine, *Tract. in Ioann. 84.*

however, has been propitiation for the world. The holy ones received but did not give crowns, and concerning the courage of the faithful, they were examples of patience rather than gifts of righteousness."[10]

Our final exception concerns reward for works: they do not depend on their merit or worth but rather on the mere kindness of God. To be sure, even our enemies confess that there is no equality between the merit of a work and its reward. But they do not consider what is special in this matter: the good works of the faithful are never so pure that they can please God without pardon. They do not consider that they are always sprinkled with some spots and blemishes, because they never flow from that full and perfect love of God that is demanded in the law. Therefore, we teach this: perfect purity is always lacking in the good works of the faithful that can endure the sight of God; on the contrary, they are even corrupt in a certain manner, if they are examined by the supreme law. But when God has once received the faithful into the grace of adoption, He not only embraces and loves their persons but also their works, so that He considers that reward worthy. In short, as it has been said about man, so we think about works: they are justified not by their own works but by the merit of Christ alone, whereas vices, which otherwise displease God, are buried in the sacrifice of Christ. This reminder is very useful to know, both to preserve people in the fear of God (lest they become prideful about their works), which proceeds from the fatherly kindness of God, and to encourage them with the greatest comfort (lest they lose heart as they regard the impurity or imperfection of their works)—to hear that they are forgiven by the fatherly indulgence of God.

The sacraments follow, in which nothing was corrected by us that our doctrine does not defend by the firmly attested authority of God. Although there were believed to have been seven established by God, we removed five from that number and demonstrated that the ceremonies were humanly devised, except marriage, which we certainly acknowledge

---

10 See Leo I, *Epist. c. 84 et 97*. Leo (c. 400–461) was bishop of Rome from 440 to 461. He is known for his *Tome*, which helped define the doctrine of Christ outlined at the Council of Chalcedon in 451.

to have been ordained by God but by no means so that it might become a sacrament. Moreover, we do not dispute about nothing when we separate the rites that were added by human counsel (even if they are otherwise neither evil nor useless) from those very holy symbols that Christ commended to us with His own mouth and the testimonies of the spiritual gifts that He willed. Just as sacraments are not in the power of men, so men cannot at all testify about them. To be sure, it is not an ordinary matter to seal the hidden kindness of God on our hearts, to offer Christ and to represent the goods that we receive in Him. Since the sacraments of Christ have this office, the failure to distinguish them from the rites advanced by men is to confuse heaven and earth. Here, however, a twofold error had prevailed: (1) having removed the distinction between divine things and human things, they greatly detracted from the holy Word of God, in which the whole power of the sacraments consists; and (2) they falsely thought that Christ was the originator of those things that have their origin from humans alone.

Similarly, we have abolished many additions to baptism that were partly useless and partly harmful because of superstition. It is known how the Apostles received the form of baptizing from Christ, how they observed it in their day, and finally how they passed it on to posterity. This simplicity, which had been established by the authority of Christ and the practice of the Apostles, did not satisfy later eras. I do not at present dispute that those who later added sacred oils, salt, spit, and candles were moved by righteous motives. I am only saying that it is hidden from no one that it came about, whether out of superstition or folly, that such additions became far more important than the truth of baptism itself. We have also been zealous to take away that misplaced confidence which regarded the external action with no consideration of Christ. For in both schools and sermons they so elevated the efficacy of the signs that they taught people, by not directing them to Christ, to trust in the visible elements. Finally, we have restored the ancient custom of administering baptism in our churches together with its doctrine. More specifically, we carefully and faithfully explain both the benefit that it brings to us and its proper practice, with the result that not even our enemies have anything to rebuke on this matter. But nothing is more foreign to the nature of the sacraments than to display an empty spectacle to the people without an explanation of the mystery. There is a well-known line that Gratian quotes from Augustine: "The water is nothing but an element, if the Word is absent."[11] Therefore, it should not seem new to our enemies, if we disapprove of a display of the sign that has been separated from the understanding of the mystery. For it is a sacrilegious divorce that overturns the rite established by Christ. And yet another vice is added in the common and otherwise familiar administration: what they regard as religion is not understood (as it is accustomed to happen in spells of magic).

But now (as I have said before) the most holy Lord's Supper, the other sacrament of the Christian church, was not only corrupted but was also nearly abolished. Therefore, it was more necessary for us to labor to purify it. First, it was necessary to pluck out of the minds of men that wicked invention that contained many absurdities. For besides that rite of religious sacrifice that had been established contrary to the clear institution of Christ, a most deadly opinion was added that that action was an atonement for sins. In this way the dignity of the priesthood, which was fit for Christ alone, was transferred to mortal men and the power of His death to their work. Hence its application flowed to the living and the dead. Therefore, in place of that fabricated sacrifice, we have restored communion, which was for the most part obsolete. For, provided that people went to the table of the Lord once a year, they thought that it was enough for the entire course of the year, if they watched what was done by the priest under the pretext of the Lord's Supper. But in this way, it happened that no trace of the supper remained there. What indeed are the words of the Lord? "Take," He says, "and distribute among yourselves."[12] But in the Mass, the pretense of offering takes the place of receiving. Indeed, there is no distribution and not even an invitation. For the priest, like a limb cut off from the rest of the body, prepares it

---

11 Gratian (twelfth century) was an Italian jurist. See *Decretum Gratiani*.
12 See 1 Corinthians 11:17–34.

for himself alone and takes it himself. How greatly do these views differ from one another! In addition, we have restored the use of the cup to the people, which, since it was not only permitted but also commended, was surely removed by no other instigator than Satan. We have abandoned a great deal of the ceremonies, partly because a multitude had grown beyond measure, and partly because some smelled too much like Judaism and others, invented by ignorant men, did not agree with the majesty of so great a mystery. But, granting that nothing else was evil than that they rashly snuck in, was it not a sufficient reason that they were removed that we noticed that the mass of men were dumbfounded by them?

Greater necessity drove us to condemn the invention of transubstantiation and the practice of preserving and carrying the bread. First of all, it contradicts the clear words of Christ, and second, it is inconsistent with the unfailing method of the sacraments. For there is no sacrament where the visible symbol is not seen, because what it symbolizes has a likeness to the spiritual truth. And what Paul says about the supper is clear: "We are all one bread and one body who are sharers of the one bread" (1 Cor. 10:17). Where is the analogy or likeness to the visible sign in the supper that corresponds to the body and blood of the Lord, if there is no bread that we eat and no wine that we drink there, but only an empty specter that deludes the eyes? Add to that the fact that a worse superstition constantly and simultaneously clings to this invention, so that people cling to the bread as if to God, and they adore it as God (as we have seen it been done). For, although a sacrament should exist as a support to direct godly minds to heaven, the world has abused the holy symbols of the supper for a contrary end—so that, content in the appearance and worship of them, they might not raise their minds to Christ. But to carry the bread in the procession or to preserve it in a more exalted place so that it may be adored is an egregious corruption foreign to the institution of Christ. For in the supper the Lord offers His body and blood to us, but so that we may eat it and drink it. Therefore, in the first place He lays down the mandate in which He bids them to receive, eat, and drink. Second, He adds and joins a promise to this, by which He testifies that what we eat is His body and what we drink is His blood. Therefore, those who either hold the bread back for worship or carry it around, since they separate the promise from the mandate, that is, they sever an unbreakable bond, imagine that they certainly have the body of Christ. But all they have is an idol that they have dreamed up for themselves. For this promise of Christ, in which He offers to us His body and blood under the symbols of the bread and the wine, applies to nobody else than those who take it from His hand, so that they practice what He commanded. But those who by their own decision turn the bread into another activity, since they lack the promise, are left with nothing but their own dream. Finally, we have restored the doctrine and explanation of the mystery that should be heard by the people. For before, the priest not only used an unknown language but also muttered with a hushed voice the words with which he thought that the bread and cup were consecrated. Here our critics have nothing to pick at except that we simply follow Christ's command. For He did not command that the bread become His body with a secret exorcism; instead, He declared with a clear voice that He gave His body to the disciples.

Meanwhile, for both baptism and the Lord's Supper we have faithfully and with as much care as possible taught the people their purpose, efficacy, benefit, and use. First of all, we exhort everybody to bring faith with which they may inwardly perceive what is represented to the eyes there, that is, the spiritual nourishment with which alone souls are fed for eternal life. We testify that the Lord promises or symbolizes nothing here in signs that He does not offer in reality. Therefore, we declare that in the supper the body and blood of Christ are both offered to us by the Lord and received by us. Moreover, we do not teach that the bread and wine are symbols without constantly adding that the truth that they signify is united to them at the same time. We are not silent about how excellent is the benefit that He renders to us from them and how our consciences have a very clear guarantee of salvation and life here. Moreover, whoever has any intellectual honesty will not deny this: among us the explanation of this mystery is heard far more clearly, and its dignity is commended in more complete statements than is usually done anywhere else.

In the government of the church we maintain only what we can establish with a very good reason. We have restored the pastoral office according to both the Apostolic rule and the custom of the ancient church, so that those who rule the church also teach. We have suggested that more diligence and caution must be applied in choosing them, and we have devoted ourselves to this. It is clear enough what sort of examination bishops carry on by their suffragans or vicars, and it is possible to draw an inference from the very fruit that it produces. For the fact that everywhere they promote idle men of no use to the office of priesthood needs no mention. Among us, even if there are ministers who are found to lack great teaching, nobody is nevertheless admitted who is not at least moderately apt to teach. The fact that all ministers are not more perfect should be attributed more to the misfortune of the times than to us. Yet we can and always will be able to justly boast this: the ministers of our churches, if compared with others, cannot appear to have been chosen carelessly. But although we are to a certain degree superior in the examination and election of ministers, we are far more eminent in this: no one holds the place of pastor among us who does not perform the office. Therefore, no church is found among us without the regular preaching of the Word of God.

Although it makes our enemies ashamed to deny this (for how could they proceed to deny a matter of such clarity?) first about the right and authority of ordaining and then about its form, they nevertheless prosecute us. They cite ancient canons that put bishops and the clergy in charge of this matter. They claim an uninterrupted succession in which this power has been handed down to them by the very hands of the Apostles. Therefore, they deny that it was lawful to be transferred to anyone else. But would that they had, by their merit, retained that property that they brag about. But if we consider now first in what order bishops have been promoted to this honor throughout the centuries, both how they conduct themselves in it and also what sort of men they tend to produce, to whom they entrust the government of the churches, we will see that that succession in which they boast was interrupted long ago. The ancient canons require that any man who is to be received into the episcopate or presbytery first be tested by a just examination of both his doctrine and life. There is very clear evidence for this matter in the acts of the Fourth African Council.[13] Furthermore, the authority to refuse or approve of a person who was nominated by a clergyman belonged to the people and the magistrate, lest anybody be forced against his will or consent. "The person who is to preside over all," says Leo in Epistle 90, "is chosen by all. For it is necessary that the person who is unknown and unexamined be appointed in such a way that he is not forced into it." Likewise, Leo says this in Epistle 87: "Let the testimony of those who are honored be regarded, as well as the subscription of the clergy and the consensus of the rank and file. There is no reason for it to be done otherwise." Cyprian[14] also asserts this very thing and quite boldly at that, affirming that it has been sanctioned by divine authority that the priest be elected, while the common people are present, before the eyes of everyone, so that he may be proven worthy and suitable by the testimony of all. This custom stood as long as the condition of the church was tolerable. For the letters of Gregory are full of proof that demonstrates that the practice was carefully observed in his time.[15]

Just as the Holy Spirit imposes the necessity of teaching on all bishops in Scripture, so in the ancient church it was similarly held as monstrous to nominate a bishop who did not at the same time show himself to be a pastor by his teaching, and no men were received into that rank under another condition. The same method prevailed for presbyters before anyone was appointed to a particular parish. Hence, those decrees: "Let them not be involved in secular matters. Let them not go very far from their congregations. Let them not be absent for a long time." It had already been sanctioned by synodical decrees that the other bishops from the whole province had to agree to ordain a bishop. But if that could not be done conveniently, no less than at least three bishops

---

13 Many synods and councils were held in North Africa in the early centuries of the church, and there is disagreement about how to number them. Calvin is probably referring to the Council of Carthage in 419.

14 Cyprian (c. 200–258) was bishop of Carthage and an influential early church father.

15 Gregory I (the Great; c. 540–604) was pope from 590 until his death.

were present. And that was done with this purpose: that nobody might usurp the office, secretly creep in, or work his way in by cunning. In the ordination of a presbyter, every bishop held a council of their presbyters. This, which could be explained at more length and confirmed more carefully in an academic treatise, I mention here only in passing because from this it will be easy to judge how much importance this smoke of succession should have, which our bishops blow in our faces to blind us.

They assert that the inheritance was bequeathed to them by the Apostles of Christ, so that they alone may put whomever they want in charge of the churches. And they complain loudly that we have usurped their power with sacrilegious rashness, because we carry on the duties of the ministry apart from their authority. How do they prove this? They succeeded the Apostles in an uninterrupted course. But is that enough, since all that is left is different? It would certainly be ridiculous to say so. In choosing them, no account is taken of their lives or doctrine. The freedom of voting was snatched away from the people. But even if the rest of the clergy is excluded, the canonical clerics drew all the power to themselves. The Roman pontiff also arrogated to himself alone ordination, which he stole from the provincial bishops. Now, as if they were elected for secular domination, they think about nothing less than carrying out the duties of the episcopate. Finally, since a conspiracy appears to have been made among them so that they may have nothing in common with the Apostles or the holy fathers of the church, they offer this pretext alone: that they have descended from them in a seamless succession. But they act as if Christ sometime taught as law that, whatever sort of lives they may live, those who are in charge of the church should be acknowledged as Apostles, or as if there were some inherited power that is transferred to the unworthy no less than to the worthy. Moreover, just as it is said of the Milesians,[16] there is caution among them lest they admit anyone who is altogether good into their company, or, if perhaps

---

16 The Milesian school was a philosophical school founded in the sixth century BC. It is most strongly associated with three philosophers from the city of Miletus, on the west coast of the Anatolian peninsula (modern-day Turkey): Thales, Anaximander, and Anaximenes.

they have admitted one by error, they will not tolerate him. I am speaking about the multitude. For I do not deny that there are a few good men among them. But either they are silent out of fear or they are not heard. Therefore, those who persecute the doctrine of Christ with iron and fire; who allow no one to speak about Christ sincerely without punishment; who block the path of truth in every way they can; who firmly resist that the church which they have knocked down will rise again; who hinder from the ministry those people who are suspected of thinking in a good and godly way about the well-being of the church; or who push out those who have already been received; it should have been expected of them that they themselves with their own hands would put in office faithful ministers who instruct the people in pure religion.

But since the expression of Gregory is used among them like a proverb, that those who abuse a privilege deserve to lose it, it is necessary either that they should be entirely different, choose others to govern the church, and take a different approach, or that they should quit complaining that they were wrongly and unjustly robbed of what rightfully belongs to them. Or, if they prefer that I speak more frankly, if they want to be acknowledged as bishops, let them arrive at the episcopate by a different approach than the one by which they arrived at it; let them be ordained by another practice and rite; and let them fulfill their office by feeding the people. In order that they may retain the authority of nominating and ordaining, let them restore that just and serious examination of doctrine and life that has now been obsolete among them for many centuries. However, let this one reason be considered as good as a thousand: whoever shows that he is actually an enemy of sound doctrine has lost all authority in the church, regardless of any sort of title that he claims for himself. It is known what the ancient councils teach about heretics and the authority that they leave for them. To be sure, they certainly forbid any of them to seek ordination. Therefore, nobody can exercise this right except the person who preserves the unity of the church with the purity of doctrine. We assert that those who preside over churches today under the name of bishops are not faithful guardians and ministers of godly doctrine, so much that instead, they are its fiercest enemies. We assert that they work hard at this alone: having made Christ extinct together with the truth of His gospel, they reinforce idolatry, ungodliness, and the worst deadly errors. We assert that they not only stubbornly attack the true doctrine of godliness with words, but also furiously rage against those who desire to draw it out of the darkness. Against so many impediments with which they fight back, we are zealous to devote our work to the church. Therefore, they lodge the complaint against us that we force our way into their property by forbidden paths.

In regard to the form or ceremony: it is a worthy matter about which they have harassed us. They do not believe that ordination is rightly done by us because of the following: we do not anoint the hands of priests, we do not blow into their faces, and we do not clothe them with white vestments or something similar. But we observe that there was once no ceremony beyond the laying on of hands. But the rest are recent customs, and do not have commendation from elsewhere except that they are now observed by the masses with intense devotion. But why is this relevant? The reason is that in such matters an authority greater than men is sought. Therefore, what has been invented by people without religion, as often as the condition of the times demands, may change. But what appeared not very long ago has far less importance. In addition, they offer a chalice and paten[17] to the hands of those priests whom they produce. Why? To initiate them in making sacrifices. But by what mandate? For Christ never entrusted His disciples with this function, and He did not want it to be undertaken by their successors. Therefore, they are out of place when they give us trouble about the form of ordaining, in which we do not at all differ from the rule of Christ, the practice of the Apostles, and the custom of the ancient church, and yet cannot defend their own position (about the neglect of which they accuse us) from the Word of God, with a firm reason, or from a pretext of antiquity.

There are laws of church government in part. We readily accept those

---

17 The chalice is the vessel that contains the Eucharistic wine, and the paten is the plate that holds the bread.

that are not also snares of consciences and that make for the preservation of public order. But we were forced to abolish those that had been imposed by tyranny to oppress consciences with bondage or that served superstition more than edification. On this topic our enemies first accuse us of fastidiousness and arrogance. Second, they charge us of pursuing license of the flesh, so that, having shaken off their yoke of discipline, we may indulge our every desire. But, as I said, we do not at all oppose any laws that are reverently preserved and that have a view to this purpose alone: that they are conducted among all the faithful decently and in order. But we do not refuse to state the reason that it was necessary to abolish every one that we abolished. It is certainly not difficult to prove that the church labored beyond measure under the burden of human traditions and that it was necessary to lighten it, if we want to consider its best interest. There is a well-known complaint of Augustine in which he seriously deplores the misfortune of his era because the church, which he wanted to be free by the mercy of God, was so oppressed at that time that the condition of the Jews was more tolerable.[18] It is likely that the number of laws has increased almost tenfold since that time. But the rigor of exacting them has increased far more. Therefore, what if that holy man were to appear again and see that infinite multitude of laws under which miserable consciences, submerged, groan? What if he were to see again the severity with which their observance is exacted? Those who rebuke us may perhaps qualify that we could have wept with Augustine if anything was displeasing, but that we should not have applied our hands for correction. There is an easy answer to this objection. For, although human laws were thought necessary to be observed, this destructive error should have been corrected. As I have said, we do not deny that laws must be diligently kept, which are endured for the sake of external polity. But to rule consciences, there is no legislator except God. Therefore, let this authority remain with Him alone, which He claims for Himself in many passages of Scripture. In that matter first, the honor of God is lessened, which is in no way lawful, and second, the spiritual freedom of

---

18 See Augustine, *Epist. 2. ad Ianuarium.*

consciences is overturned, which Paul especially forbids to be subjected to the will of men. Therefore, because it belonged to our duty to release the consciences of the faithful from unjust bondage in which they were tightly bound, we have taught that they have been set free and liberated from the laws of men. This freedom, which was obtained by the blood of Christ, must not be prostituted. If anyone makes us liable for this reason, it is necessary that he also drag into the same liability both Christ and the Apostles. And I cannot yet elaborate the other evils that they forced us to introduce as human traditions. I will only mention two, which, having been heard, I trust that all readers will be equally content. First, several of them, since they exceeded human capability, could lead people to nothing else than hypocrisy or despair. But second, everything had come into practice for which Christ rebuked the Pharisees, so that because of them God's commands became ineffective.

I will now bring up examples in which that will be made more clear. There are three matters about which they are especially angry at us: (1) we have allowed freedom to eat meats on any day; (2) we have permitted marriage to priests; (3) we have done away with private confession that was made in the ear of the priest. Let the enemies respond to me in good faith: Is not a person who has eaten meat on Friday more harshly punished among them than the person who regularly visits prostitutes throughout the whole course of the year? Or, is it not regarded as a deadlier crime if a priest takes a wife than if he were caught in adultery a hundred times? Or, do they not more readily ignore it if somebody despises the many commands of God than if he has neglected to confess his sins into the ear of a priest once a year? How monstrous is it, I ask, that it appears as a minor vice and worthy of pardon if someone violates the most holy law of God, but that if someone breaks the precepts of men, it is regarded as an evil deed that cannot be atoned for? To be sure, I confess that this is not a new example. For, as I have said, Christ accuses the Pharisees of this wickedness: they make the commandments of God ineffective because of their own traditions (Matt. 15:6). But this is that arrogance of the Antichrist about which Paul speaks: he sits in the temple of God, parading himself as God (2 Thess. 2:4). Where indeed is the incomparable majesty of God, after mortal man has come to the point that his laws are preferred to the eternal decrees of God? I am omitting that the Apostle calls the prohibition of foods and marriage the doctrine of demons (1 Tim. 4:3). Surely in that there is more than enough evil. But this is the highest heap of wickedness: to put man in a higher rank than God. If they deny that what I am saying is true, I challenge them to disprove me.

Now, what else are those two laws about celibacy and auricular confession than terrible murderers of souls? The purpose is that all ministers of the churches take a vow of perpetual chastity. After the vow has been taken, it is never lawful for them to take wives. What if someone deprived of the gift of self-control burns with passion? They say that there is no place for exception here. But experience shows that it has prevailed more that this yoke is never placed on priests than so that those who are restricted burn with a constant fire in the furnace of their lusts. The enemies recount the praises of virginity and the conveniences of celibacy, by which they prove that marriage was not rashly forbidden to priests. They even plead that it is right and honorable. But by all this, will they prove that it is permitted to throw snares onto consciences, which Christ not only left unburdened and free, but also set free by His authority and at the cost of His own blood? Paul does not dare to do this (1 Cor. 7:35). Therefore, where does this new license come from? Moreover, why does the whole world stink of this obscenity for the celibacy of the priests, so that virginity is carried into heaven with praises? If they actually displayed the chastity that they profess in word, I would perhaps allow them to say that it is fitting for this to be done. But since nobody now knows that the prohibition of marriage is for priests a license to visit prostitutes, by what front, I ask, do they dare to make any mention of propriety? But since their disgrace is not well known, lest it be necessary for me to dispute with them for a long time, I refer them to the tribunal of God, so that they may discuss their chastity there. Someone may qualify that the law is imposed on nobody except the person who takes the vow of his own free will. But what greater necessity can be conceived than when they force them to take the vow? This condition is required of everyone, lest anyone be admitted to the rank of priest who has not himself first bound himself by oath to perpetual celibacy. The person who has taken the vow is also forced against his will to fulfill what he once received, and no excuse to the contrary will be listened to. Later, they say that celibacy that is demanded in this way is voluntary. But whatever inconveniences and conveniences of celibacy they may recount must be granted to rhetoricians, so that by declaiming about these matters in the schools they may practice their speaking. But whatever was said should not be so important that miserable souls are therefore entangled in a deadly snare, with which they must constantly struggle until they have been strangled. And yet among such shameful baseness even hypocrisy still has a place. For whatever sort of men they may be, they nevertheless regard themselves as better because they lack wives. The reason for confession is the same. For they derive uses that follow from it. We, on the contrary, are no less ready to point out the many dangers that must rightly be feared and to refer to the very many serious harms that flow from it.

Let me say that these are arguments about which it is possible for both sides to dispute. But the rule of Christ is perpetual, and it can neither be changed nor twisted here or there. Even more, it is unlawful to stir controversy about this, lest consciences be oppressed into bondage. In fact, such a law is what they promote, so that it cannot but torment souls and at last strangle them. For it requires that each person confess all his sins once a year to his own priest; if that does not happen, it leaves him no hope of obtaining pardon. Those who are seriously experienced, that is, who have braved the danger with the true fear of God, know that not even 1 percent is possible. For they could not provide themselves with any remedy other than to drive people to despair. But for those who somewhat wanted to satisfy God otherwise, confession was a very suitable veil for hypocrisy. For because they believed that they were finished before the tribunal of God, as soon as they had shaken off their sins into the ear of the priest, they dared to sin more freely because the method of releasing them was so expedient. Next, because this conviction sunk deep in their souls—that they were doing what the law commanded—they thought that they included all their sins in their every confession; but they did not even account for a thousandth of them. Behold, why our enemies cry out that the discipline of the church was destroyed by us: we were zealous to relieve wounded consciences, lest they perish, being oppressed by a most cruel tyranny. And we have drawn hypocrites out of their hiding places into the open light, so that they might examine themselves more closely and begin to think better of the judgment of God, which they were secretly fleeing before.

But someone will say that, however many abuses there were that were worthy of correction, the laws nevertheless being holy, useful, and in a certain manner already consecrated for a long time, it was thus not necessary for them to be completely abolished immediately. Regarding the eating of meats, I respond nothing else than that we have the doctrine that accords with the ancient church, in which it is known that one was always free to eat meats or to abstain from them. I confess that the prohibition of marriage for priests is ancient, and so is the vow of perpetual chastity for monks and nuns. But if they grant that the certain will of God outweighs human custom, why do they bring charges against us concerning antiquity, even though it agrees with us and it is by no means a secret that it clearly supports us? The sentence is clear: "Let marriage be regarded as honorable among all" (Heb. 13:4). And Paul expressly attributed wives to bishops (1 Tim. 3:2; Titus 1:6). But on the whole, he calls to marriage everyone who burns (1 Cor. 7:9), and he declares that the prohibition of marriage is the doctrine of demons (1 Tim. 4:3). What advantage is there to setting human custom against such clear words of the Holy Spirit other than to prefer men to God?

Moreover, it is worth noting how unfair the judges are who set the practice of the ancient church against us on this matter. For what antiquity of the church is more ancient or more worthy of authority than the one under the Apostles? But our enemies will not deny that marriage was permitted and practiced at that time by all the ministers of the church. If the Apostles thought it good to prohibit priests from marriage, why did they deprive the church of such a good thing? After that, about 250 years passed until the Council of Nicaea. Sozomen relates that in the council the question of imposing celibacy on ministers was certainly considered, but when Paphnutius protested against it, the whole matter was dissolved.[19] For, since he (himself being celibate) denied that the law of celibacy should be tolerated, Sozomen recounts that the whole council readily agreed with him. But as superstition gradually increased, the law that had been rejected at that time was accepted at last. One canon existed among those that are attributed to the Apostles (not so much because of their antiquity as because of the uncertainty of the authors) that did not permit clergy to take wives, excepting only singers and readers, after they were elected into office. But in another older canon priests and deacons are prohibited to refuse wives under the pretext of religion. And in the fourth chapter of the Council of Gangra, anathema is pronounced against those who distinguished a married presbyter from others, so that under this pretext they may keep themselves away from his offering. Hence, it is apparent that in those times there was still to some extent more fairness than a later age would have.

And yet it is not my plan here to exhaust this whole affair in an academic disputation. It seemed fitting, however, to indicate (only in passing) that the first and very pure church is not so much against us here as our enemies pretend. But even if we were to grant that to them, why do they nevertheless so cruelly accuse us, as if we mixed the sacred with the profane? But they act as if it is not easy to answer back (against them) that we agree with the ancient church far more than they do. We make marriage, which the ancients denied to those priests, free. How will they respond to me about visiting prostitutes, which has prevailed among them everywhere? They will deny that they approve of it. But if they wanted to comply with the ancient canons, it would be necessary to chastise it more harshly. The Council of Neocaesarea established the penalty that a priest must abdicate from office, if he takes a wife.[20] But if he commits adultery or visits a prostitute, it punishes far more severely, so that, being deposed

---

19 Sozomen (fifth century) wrote a history of the church that covered the period from 323 to 425. Paphnutius (d. c. 360) is noted for persuading the Council of Nicaea not to impose celibacy on ministers.

20 The Council of Neocaesarea was held in Cappadocia in the early fourth century.

from his office, he is also excommunicated. If anyone takes a wife now, it is regarded as a deadly sin; if, however, he visits a hundred prostitutes, he is fined with the smallest sum of money. Add to that the fact that if those who first introduced the law of celibacy were alive today, taught by present experience they would undoubtedly be the first to abolish it. As I said, however, it would be too unjust for us to be condemned by human authority when we are plainly freed by the Word of God.

Our defense concerning confession is briefer and more expedient. For our enemies will not show that any necessity of confessing was imposed on the faithful before Innocent III.[21] Therefore, this tyranny for which they so bitterly attack us was not known to the Christian world for 1,200 years. But there is a decree of the Lateran Council (as there are many others of the same sort). People who are moderately knowledgeable of history know that ignorance and barbarism characterized those times. And it usually happens that the more unlearned those who rule are, the more tyrannical they are. Otherwise, all godly souls will be my witnesses that it is necessary that they are trapped in a labyrinth of sorts who think that they are bound by that law. A blasphemous arrogance was added to such cruel torture of consciences: they confined the forgiveness of sins there. For they pretended that nobody had the pardon of God except who had the desire to confess. What indeed is this, that men design a method in their own head in which a sinner is reconciled to God, so that while God offers pardon simply, they deny it until the condition that they have added has been fulfilled? From another angle, this most terrible superstition gripped the people: as soon as they had unloaded their sins into the ear of the priest, they were free from all guilt. Many people abused this false opinion for a looser license to sin. Moreover, even those equipped with a greater fear of God still looked more to the priest than to Christ. Otherwise, the public and solemn confession, as Cyprian says, that used to be imposed on repentant people when they were about to be reconciled to the church, no sane person fails to praise and embrace, provided

---

21 Innocent III (1160–1216) served as the pope who presided over the Fourth Lateran Council in 1215.

that it be directed to no other end than the one for which it was established. Finally, on this subject there is no disagreement between us and the ancient church; instead, we only want the tyranny that arose not so long ago to be torn away from the necks of the faithful, as is just. In addition, if anyone, in order that he may be assisted with comfort and counsel, privately approaches his minister and intimately pours out his heart to him—the reasons for his anxiety—we by no means deny that it may be done in a godly and useful way, provided that it does not become a necessity rather than a liberty. Let this liberty be left to each person, so that he may do what he knows is best for him. Let the conscience of nobody be bound to certain laws. I hope, O Caesar, that this defense satisfies both your majesty and you, O most illustrious princes, as it is entirely fair.

But however justly we deplore that the doctrine of the truth was corrupted and that all of Christianity was defiled by many vices, our critics nevertheless deny that in addition there was a reason that it was necessary that the church be so disturbed and that the whole world be shaken up in a certain manner. To be sure, we are neither so stupid that we do not think that public uproars should be carefully guarded against nor so hard-hearted that we are not moved and even shudder with our whole hearts when we notice this confused condition of the church. But by what fairness is the blame of the present movements attributed to us, since they were certainly not stirred up by us? More specifically, by what front do they indict us for having disturbed the church who (it is agreed) are the authors of all the uproars? In other words, it is the wolves who are complaining about the lambs. When Luther emerged in the beginning, he lightly noted (and that with moderation) only a few abuses—both excessively crass ones and ones no longer tolerable—more so that he might indicate that he desired them to be corrected than dare to correct them himself. This immediately sounded a call to arms from the enemy, and when the tension was raised more and more, our enemy thought that this was the best solution: to suppress the truth with force and brutality. And so when our men challenged them to friendly disputation and wanted the disagreements to be settled by peaceful methods, they cruelly oppressed us with bloodthirsty edicts until the matter was brought to that wretched dispersion.

Yet this false accusation is not new. What we are forced to hear now the wicked Ahab also once reproached Elijah for, namely that he disturbed Israel. But the holy prophet acquitted us with his response: "I am not doing so, but you and the house of your father are. For you have abandoned the Lord and have gone after Baals" (1 Kings 18:17–18). Therefore, it is not just that we are subjected to hatred today because such a fierce struggle about religion rages among Christians, unless they first want to condemn Elijah, with whom we have the same defense. He defended himself with this argument alone: he fought for nothing else than to vindicate the glory of God and restore the pure worship of Him, but he threw back the charge of the uproars and struggles at those who were in an uproar to resist the truth. But why else have we acted so far, and why do we act now also, except so that God alone may be worshiped among us and His simple truth may reign in the church? If our enemies deny this, it is at least fitting that we be convicted of wicked doctrine before it is turned against us as vice that we dissent from others. For what were we supposed to do? There was one condition of obtaining peace—that by being silent we might betray the truth. It would not have been sufficient, however, to remain silent, unless we had approved with a silent consensus wicked doctrine, open blasphemies against God, and the worst superstitions. Therefore, what else could we do than at least testify with a clear voice that we are strangers to participation in godlessness? Therefore, we simply devoted ourselves to do what belonged to our duty. Furthermore, the matter that has broken out into such hostile discord is an evil to be blamed on those who have preferred to mix heaven with earth rather than to give place to godly, sound doctrine, so that they might also retain the tyranny they just usurped.

Although this should be more than enough for our defense (for the most holy truth of God stands on our side, and by asserting it we only check the struggle), our enemies, nevertheless, by fighting with us, do not so much wage war against us as against God Himself. Next, because we stooped to this heat of controversies not of our own will but by the intemperance of those who do not share our opinion, we were forced into it. Whatever happened, there is no reason that we should be subjected to hatred. For, just as it does not belong to us to control events, so it does not belong to us to be responsible for them. This is old and practiced in every age: that the wicked take the opportunity to cause uproar and later impose this disgrace on the gospel, as if it provided the cause for the dissension which (even when it has not been offered to them) they seize upon in their depravity. And just as it was necessary that that prophecy be fulfilled that Christ was to His own people a stone of stumbling and a rock of offense in the first church, so it is no wonder that it is also true in our time. Certainly this must be regarded as astonishing: that the architects reject the stone that should hold first place in the foundation. But because this was done to Christ from the beginning, let us not be shocked when it also comes into use today. Here I appeal to your majesty, O Caesar, and to your greatness, O princes, when this unfortunate dispersion and other infinite evils that sprung from dissension enter your thoughts or are mentioned by the word of men, may it at the same time enter your mind that Christ was appointed for opposition—so that as often as His gospel is preached, it immediately excites the rage of the wicked to war. Now, it is necessary that shaking be made out of the conflict. Therefore, this has been the perpetual condition of the gospel from when it first sprang up and always will be until the end: the world receives the preaching of it with great strife. But it belongs to prudence to notice from where the cause of this evil is born. Everybody who considers this will easily release us from all blame. It was certainly necessary for us to bear witness to the truth, as we did. Woe to the world if it prefers to invoke Christ for controversy rather than to embrace the peace offered by Him. For undoubtedly the person will be humbled who will not endure correction from Him.

But this again is objected against us: that not all the vices of the church should be corrected with such harsh remedies, that they should not be painfully exacted, and not even to all should healing be applied; instead, some should be gently chastised and others tolerated if change does not pose any difficulty. I respond that we are not so inexperienced in common life that we do not know that the church has always been (and always will be) liable to some vices that certainly must be rejected by the godly but that must be endured rather than bitterly fought over for their sake. Otherwise, our enemies do harm to us when they accuse us of excessive pedantry, as if we have caused trouble for the church because of trivial and light errors. For they also add this charge to the others, diminishing with as much cunning as possible the things about which we stir up controversy: that we appear to be driven more by lust for quarreling than by a just cause. Indeed, they do not do that out of ignorance but from learned counsel. For they know that nothing is more hateful than the kind of inconsiderateness that they attribute to us. Yet they also advance their own ungodliness because they speak so contemptuously about the greatest things of all. But is it the case that, when we complain that the worship of God had been defiled; when His honor had been entirely diminished; when the doctrine of salvation had been entangled in so many destructive errors; when the excellence of Christ had been buried; finally, when everything holy was defiled by sacrileges; they deride our folly, as if we harassed the whole world in vain by disputing about trifling questions? But because these cannot quickly be touched upon, the place demands that I explain to you more carefully the dignity and weight of those things about which we contend, so that it may be apparent not only that they should not have been neglected but also that they could not have been overlooked by us, lest we had been entangled in a very great evil and wicked faithlessness toward God. This was the third of the three heads that I said I would speak about in the beginning. I would like to know, first of all, by what front they dare to call themselves Christians who charge us with having rashly disturbed the church with quarrels for very insignificant reasons. For if they were to make our religion as significant as the ancient idolaters made theirs, they would not thus reproach devotion to preserving it, which they were considered to prefer to all other cares and matters. For when the ancient idolaters said that they fought for their altars and hearths, they seem to attribute to themselves the greatest and most favorable cause of all. To those today the contention that is raised for the glory of God and the salvation of men seems to be almost unnecessary. For we do not quarrel about the shadow of a donkey, as it has been said, but the whole sum of the Christian religion is called into question. If nothing else were to come into account, would the eternal and inviolable truth of God—which renders so many clear testimonies certain and for the confirmation of which so many holy prophets and so many martyrs met death, of which the Son of God Himself was a preacher and witness and which He finally sealed with His blood—be of so little value to us that it should be trampled underfoot while we watch and remain silent?

But I am giving way to details. We know how damnable a thing idolatry is to God, and history everywhere tells us how He avenged it with dreadful punishments among both the Israelite people and other nations. We hear the same vengeance declared from His own mouth in every age. For He speaks to us when He swears by His holy name that He will not tolerate His glory to be given to idols and when He testifies that He is jealous, who will avenge to the third and fourth generation all sins and this very one before the others. This is the sin, for the sake of which Moses, a man of an otherwise gentle character, inflamed by the Spirit of God, commanded the Levites to run in different directions throughout the camp and consecrate the hands of their brothers with blood (Ex. 32:27); for the sake of which God again and again punished His people and afflicted on them plagues, famine, the sword, and finally, every kind of misfortune; for the sake of which the very powerful kingdom of Israel first fell and then that of Judah; the holy city of Jerusalem was forgotten; the temple of God that was singular on earth at the time was destroyed; the people who had been specially chosen out of all peoples, to whom God united Himself with covenant, who alone bore the distinguishing marks of God, who lived under His protection and dominion, finally from whom Christ was born, was afflicted in every way, stripped of all its dignity, driven into exile, and nearly brought to destruction. It would take a long time to recount everything here. There is no page in the Prophets that does not shout that there is nothing that provokes God more to indignation. What, then? When we saw that open idolatry prevailed everywhere in the world, should we have winked at it? But to have done that would have been to gently stroke the world, asleep in its own destruction, lest it be awakened.

Let the very many corruptions enter your mind, O most invincible Caesar and most illustrious princes, with which it is first demonstrated that the worship of God was defiled. You will truly find that a certain deluge of ungodliness overflowed, as it were, whereby the whole of religion was suffocated. Hence, divine honors were displayed for statues, men were praying to them everywhere, and they were imagining that the divinity and power of God were under them. Hence dead saints were worshiped no differently than Baals also once were among the Israelites. And very many other measures were devised by the cunning of Satan by which God's glory was dismembered. The Lord cries out that He burns with jealousy if anything is set up as an idol, and Paul demonstrates by his own example that His servants should be no less zealous for promoting His glory (Acts 17:16). Moreover, that zeal for the house of God, which should consume the hearts of all the faithful, is not common. Therefore, since God's glory was so defiled or rather mangled, would we not be faithless by winking at and being silent before it? If a dog sees any violence inflicted on its owner, it will immediately bark. Shall we look on silently while God's holy name is violated by so many sacrileges? Then where would be the place for this: "The reproaches of those who reproach You have fallen upon me" (Ps. 69:9)?

But who was allowed to silently overlook that mockery in which God was worshiped not otherwise than by the outward gesture and foolish inventions of men? We know how much He hates hypocrisy. What was practiced everywhere reigned in that fabricated worship of God. We hear the severity of words with which all the prophets inveighed against worship devised by the rashness of men. Good intention, that is, an insane lust for daring anything, was thought the best rule for worshiping God. Certainly out of all the worship of God, as it had been established, there was almost nothing that bore witness to the Word of God. Here it is not the case that we stand on our own judgment or on that of others. But the voice of God must be heard, in which He testifies how much He regards this worship as a profanation of Him—when men run riot in their own inventions beyond the boundaries of His Word. He gives two reasons that He punishes the blinded Israelite people, deprived of a godly and holy government of the church: hypocrisy and will-worship (ἐθελοθρησκείαν), that is, a humanly devised form of worshiping Him. As Isaiah 29:13–14 says, "Because this people approached Me with their lips, but their heart was far from Me, and because they worshiped Me by the commandments of men, behold, I will declare a dreadful omen, at the hearing of which all will be astounded. Wisdom will indeed depart from the wise, and prudence will vanish from the elders." A similar or greater perversion openly reigned in the churches when God stirred us up. When God thundered from heaven, should we have been silent?

Perhaps they will consider that it was a light error that it became a custom for solemn prayers to be made in churches in an unknown language, against the clear prohibition of God. But since it is apparent that God was mocked in that way, they will not deny that we had more than a sufficiently just cause for crying out against them. What about those blasphemies that were resounding in the public hymns, which no godly person can bear to hear without greatly shuddering? Those epithets for Mary are observed when they call her the gate of heaven, hope, life, and salvation. And they were carried forward with such furor and madness that they attributed to her the right to command Christ. Indeed, that damnable and wicked song is still heard in many churches: "Ask the Father and command the Son." In no less moderate expressions of praise do they worship certain saints and certainly their own, that is, whom they have entered into the catalog of saints by their own opinion. For, among the very many praises that they sing to Claudius, they call him a light for the blind, a road for wanderers, and life and resurrection for the dead.[22] The formulas for prayer that they have in daily use must be attributed to such blasphemies. The Lord declares very severe punishments against those who mix His name with the names of Baals, whether in oaths or in prayers. Therefore, what punishment hangs over our heads, who not only mix saints (as lesser gods) with Him, but who, with insult to His honor, strip Christ of His own singular titles with which He adorned

---

22 Probably Claudius of Besançon (c. 607–96/98), known as Claude the Thaumaturge, a French priest, monk, abbot, and bishop.

Him, so that we may confer them on creatures? Should we have also been silent about this, so that by faithless silence we would have also summoned against ourselves such a grave judgment?

I remain silent that nobody was praying to God with certain faith, that is, sincerely, and that nobody was even able to do so. For while Christ was buried in this manner, as He was, it was necessary that people constantly doubt God's fatherly kindness toward them—whether He wanted to bring them help or had concern for their salvation. What? Was it a trivial or tolerable error that the eternal priesthood of Christ, as if made available for plunder, was conferred to any of the saints? We have noted that Christ procured this honor for Himself by His death, so that He is the eternal advocate and peacemaker, who presents us and our prayers to the Father, obtains for us favor with Him, and makes for us the hope of obtaining what we seek. Just as He alone both died for us and redeemed us by His death, so He allows no sharing of this honor. Therefore, what sacrilege is filthier than that which our enemies promptly have in their mouths—that Christ is indeed the only mediator of redemption, but all the saints are mediators of intercession? Is not Christ thus left without glory, as if, having discharged the office of priest once in death, He has now transferred it to the saints? Or should we have been silent at that time when the special majesty of Christ, established at so great a cost, was snatched away from Him by a supreme insult, as if it were enemy plunder divided among the saints? But by speaking in this way, they do not deny that Christ intercedes for us even now, provided that we understand that He does so together with the saints, namely as any one of Christ's people. But Christ acquired distinguished honor for Himself with His blood, if this alone followed as a consequence: that He would be an associate of Hugo or Lubin or anyone else from the lowest dregs of the saints whom the Roman pontiff has created by his will.[23] To be sure, it is not asked here whether they also pray, about which matter

---

23 Hugo was probably Hugh of Cluny (1024–1109), abbot of the monastery in Cluny and an influential figure in the eleventh-century Roman Catholic Church. Lubin was probably Leobinus (d. 556), a hermit, a priest, abbot of Brou, and bishop of Chartres.

there is nothing more sufficient to know than that Scripture makes no mention of it. But this is the matter about which we contend: whether Christ—overlooked, regarded negligently, or entirely dismissed—allows us to look to the saints for protection. Or, if someone prefers more specificity, the question is whether Christ alone is priest—who opens the sanctuary of God the Father for us and leads us there by the hand, and by His supplication He turns the Father to hear our prayers and pardon us for His protection—and in our prayers we should plead His name, or He maintains this office together with other saints.

I showed above that Christ was for the most part deprived not only of the honor of priesthood but also of the grace for all His benefits. For certainly He is called redeemer, but so that men may also redeem themselves from the bondage to sin and death by free will. Certainly He is called righteousness and salvation, but so that men may acquire for themselves salvation by the merits of their own works. Indeed, on this point nothing makes the scholastics ashamed to restrict that inestimable benefit of redemption, for the narration of which no eloquence of men or angels is sufficient, so that they say that He conferred on us the first merit that they call the occasion for meriting, but that we, helped by this aid, merit eternal life by our own works. To be sure, they confess that we were washed from our sins by the blood of Christ but so that everyone may hence wash himself clean. To be sure, the death of Christ has the title of sacrifice, but so that sins may be atoned for by the daily sacrifices of men. To be sure, Christ is said to have reconciled us to God the Father, but the condition is added that men pay back the penalties required by the judgment of God with their own satisfactions. When help is sought from the benefit of the keys, no more honor is held for Christ than for Cyprian or Cyricius.[24] For they simultaneously mix together the merits of the martyrs and Christ, so that they may use up the treasury of the church. Do we not hear here as many words as damnable blasphemies, with which the glory of Christ is torn apart and mangled, so that He

---

24 Cyricius was probably Cyricus (d. 304), also known as Saint-Cyr, a French child who according to tradition was martyred along with his mother, Julitta, in Tarsus.

Himself, almost emptied, retains the name alone but lacks the power? Should we also have remained silent here, when we decided to bring it into order, so that the Son of God, upon whom the Father conferred all authority, power, and glory, and in whom alone He commands us to boast, might be a little more eminent over His servants? When we saw that His benefits were thrown into oblivion; when His excellence was buried by the ingratitude of men; when the cost of His blood became worthless; when the benefit of His death was nearly abolished; finally, when He was so disfigured by the false and filthy opinions of men, that He was more like an empty specter than Himself, should we have endured this silently and quietly? O how wretched the patience, when the honor of God is diminished (not to say prostrate), if we tread so lightly that we can look the other way and wink at it! O how the benefits of Christ were wrongly obtained for us, if we thus tolerate their memory to be suffocated by wicked blasphemies!

I return again to the second part of Christian doctrine. Who will deny that everywhere people are so deluded that they think that they earn eternal life by the merit of works? I confess that for the time being they join the grace of God to their own works, but since they are confident that they are not otherwise pleasing to Him than if they are worthy, it is clear that their trust and boasting resides in works. This is the well-known and most received doctrine in all schools, and the opinion deeply implanted in the souls of nearly all people: as a person is worthy, so he is loved by God. Having accepted this, are not souls raised to a height by a devilish confidence, so that later they fall down from a very heavy precipice into an abyss of despair? Why do they want to earn God's favor not even with true obedience but with unsuitable works of no value? Indeed, these are regarded as primary among meritorious works: to whisper many little prayers; to build altars, statues, or tables to set there; to frequent churches; to run from church to church; to hear many Masses; to buy some; I do not know by what forms of abstinence, which differ entirely from Christian fasting, they afflict their bodies and diligently rely on keeping the traditions of men. Is there not still more madness in satisfactions, since they sought by the expiatory custom of the gentiles to reconcile themselves to God with them? For while they were doing everything with a doubtful and trembling conscience, that terrible anxiety was constantly coming upon them, or rather that dire torment about which I have already spoken. For they were commanded to doubt whether they were exceedingly hateful to God with their own works. Furthermore, trust having been overturned in this way, it is necessary at the same time for what Paul said to happen: that the promise of the eternal inheritance be abolished. Where, then, was the salvation of men? But if we had been silent when there was such great necessity to speak out, we would have been not only ungrateful and unfaithful toward God but also inhumane toward humans, over all of whom we see eternal destruction hanging—except those who were led back to the way.

If a dog should see its owner inflicted with as much harm as the outrage that is inflicted in the sacraments, it would bark immediately, and it would rather put its own life in danger than silently allow its owner to be treated badly in this way. Should we show less obedience to God than a beast usually does to a person? I remain silent that, the mysteries having been established by Christ and commended by His heavenly authority, they made the rites advanced by the mere authority of men equal which, however, itself deserved to be sharply rebuked. But when the mysteries themselves were corrupted by so many superstitions, polluted by so many depraved opinions that we have refuted, prostituted for the disgraceful and disreputable gain without any shame, should we have pretentiously tolerated it? Christ drove the money changers out of the temple with a whip, overturned their tables with His hand, and drove out the merchants. I admit that it is not permitted to everyone to take a whip in the hand, but it is fitting for all those who profess to belong to Christ to burn with that zeal with which Christ was stirred to vindicate the glory of the Father. Consequently, what has shown to displease Him so greatly in the polluted work of the church at least belongs to us to condemn boldly with a free and firm voice. Who is ignorant of the fact that what is for sale has now been for a long time no less holy in churches than what the merchants offer for sale in the middle of the market? And indeed, some sell at a price settled with others, after they bargain for a bid. But since in the supper more than in the rest, the example is quite clear and has more shamefulness, come now, with what conscience could we have winked at so many sacrileges and so many defilements of Him? Since words are now failing me to express these things, by what law did it become vice for us to inveigh against them, so that we were too vehement?

Here I implore you, O most invincible Caesar and most illustrious princes, by the holy body of Christ, which He offered to be sacrificed for us, that by venerating the blood that He shed for our purification, you may consider how important the mystery should be in which that body is displayed to us for food and that blood for drink—by what religion and by what care it should be preserved undefiled. Therefore, to what ingratitude will it belong, if anyone watches this heavenly mystery that Christ commended to us in the likeness of the costliest pearl being trampled on by the feet of pigs and remains silent? But we saw that it is not only trampled on but corrupted with every sort of defilement. What sort of mockery was it that the efficacy of Christ's death was converted into a human theatrical performance? That the sacrifice-offering priest, as Christ's successor, set himself up as mediator between God and men? That, the power of the one sacrifice having been buried, a thousand sacrifices were daily offered in one city to atone for sins? That Christ was sacrificed a thousand times a day, as if it were not sufficient that He died once for us? They abused the title of the most Holy Supper by inflicting all those insults on Christ, if indeed all are contained in the name of sacrifice alone. But I am not ignorant of the interpretations that the enemy now alleges to remove such absurdities. But since the abominations that I have so far related are all shamelessly practiced—now that they have been exposed—they dig up new rabbit holes for themselves, with which they nevertheless by no means hide their disgrace. They have taught that the Mass is a sacrifice in which sins might be atoned for, not only for the living, but also for the dead. What do they gain now by finding excuses, except advancing their own shamelessness? How great also is the defilement of the sacrament, because although the lawful consecration is established in the clear preaching of the Word, the bread is consecrated with a blow and a whisper? Because it is not distributed in the assembly of the faithful, but is eaten separately by one person or is put aside for another use? Because, although some distribution is made, the people are deprived of half of it, that is, the cup, contrary to the clear prohibition of the Lord? What sort of madness is it that they imagine that the substance of the bread is abolished by their exorcisms, so that it is changed into Christ? What sort of disgrace is it that selling of the Masses is practiced no more bashfully than that of shoes? For if what they say is accepted, that is, they sell the merit of Christ's death, certainly they make no lighter an insult to Christ than if they had spit in His face.

O most invincible Caesar and most illustrious princes, let it enter your mind what once befell the Corinthians because of one—not so grave at first sight—abuse of this sacrament. Each person was taking his own dinner at home, not so that they may take it together in common, but so that the rich might feast luxuriously but that the poor might go hungry. Paul declares that it was for this reason that they were chastised by the Lord with a fierce and furious plague; he admonished, nevertheless, that this was a fatherly whip with which He would call them to repentance (1 Cor. 11:30). Hence, you gather, what must be expected of us today, who have not swerved just a little bit from the right institution of Christ but have departed from it with a gigantic interval. We have corrupted its purity not in one instance but in very many, and certainly we have disfigured it with those terrible measures. We have disturbed its lawful use not only with one abuse but have overturned the whole administration. But there is no doubt that God began to avenge this wickedness long ago. The world has already for many continuous years been weighed down with many various hardships and misfortunes, and now it has nearly come to the extremity of misery. Certainly we are either astounded at our wounds or dream up other reasons that God thus afflicts us. But if we consider how light that error was by which the Corinthians defiled the Lord's Supper in comparison with the very many corruptions with which today it is defiled and corrupted, it is a wonder if we do not acknowledge that God, who so severely punished them, is justly angrier at us.

If I wanted to pursue how shameful the corruption of church government is, I would enter an infinite forest. Here I am refraining from speaking about the life of priests for many reasons. Everyone can ponder for himself that these three vices must not be tolerated: (1) that, the order of the just calling having been removed, priesthoods everywhere are occupied by force, simony,[25] fraud, or by other improper and evil arts; (2) that those who rule are empty shadows or dead effigies rather than true ministers in regard to discharging their office; (3) finally, that although they should govern consciences by the Word of God, they oppress them with unjust tyranny and hold them bound tightly by many chains of wicked laws. Is it that, not only the laws of God and of men having been rejected, but also all shame having been abandoned, a filthy confusion reigns in promoting bishops and presbyters, the lust for rule prevails, simony is rarely absent, and, as if these evils were trifling, correction is postponed to a future age? Now, when the concern for teaching lies prostrate, what kind of ministry is still left? Now, for the spiritual freedom of consciences, we see how many struggles Paul endured and how great was the contention that he stirred up. But the person who judges with fairness truly understands that we have more than enough just reasons for contending now. Therefore, in so great a distortion of all godly doctrine, in such a wicked defilement of the sacraments, in such a deplored calamity of the church, those who deny that we should have been so vehemently stirred up could not have been satisfied otherwise than if we had advanced the worship of God, the glory of Christ, the salvation of men, and the whole administration of holy matters and of the church with faithless patience. The term *moderation* is lovely, and tolerance is a beautiful and praiseworthy virtue, but the rule must be kept all the way to the altars, that is, lest we patiently allow the holy name of God to be cut to pieces by wicked blasphemies, His eternal truth to be suffocated by lies of the devil, Christ to be spit upon, His mysteries to be defiled, poor souls to be cruelly killed, and the church to be lethally wounded to grapple with final destruction. For this would not be gentleness but indifference to those things that must be regarded as of primary importance.

---

25 Simony is the buying and selling of church offices and relics. It is named after Simon Magus (see Acts 8:9–24).

So far I am confident that I have sufficiently demonstrated what I proposed: that in correcting the vices of the church we were by no means more vehement than the thing itself demanded. And that has not escaped those who censure us. Therefore, they take refuge in another accusation: that by making a disturbance we achieved nothing else than the result that the Christian world burns with warring intestines, which was at peace before. Indeed, they claim that no change appears, so that everything has fallen for the worse, saying that among those who have embraced our doctrine, few have become better from it, so that even some, if not the majority, have shown audacity for more careless wickedness. In addition, they object that there is no discipline in our churches, no laws for abstinence, no practice of humility, and that the layperson, who is held back by no yoke, runs riot in license without penalty. Finally, they envy us for plundering church goods. For they claim that our princes pounced on that and no differently than for enemy plunder, so that the church, unworthy of violence, was plundered, and today, having confused the distinction, take possession of the inheritance of the church from those who have occupied it in the midst of the noisy contentions without right and without any honest title.

To be sure, I do not deny that when wickedness reigned apart from controversy, its kingdom was disturbed by us. But if sound, godly doctrine immediately also shined on the world when everybody who willingly and with eager hearts gave us a hand, as was right, there would be no less tranquil peace and quiet today among all the churches, while Christ's reign flourishes, than at that time when the Antichrist was maintaining tyranny. Therefore, let those who hinder the course of the truth cease to wage war with Christ, and there will immediately be the greatest concord, or let them cease to throw back at us the blame for the quarrels that they themselves stir up. For surely it is very evil that they undertake to obtain no other condition of peace by themselves except that, the doctrine of godliness having been finished off, just as Christ was hidden in the tomb, the Antichrist will conquer the church again, not only to boast of innocence but to insult us in addition. We who desire nothing else than unity, for the rule of which the eternal truth of God is a bond,

have endured every accusation and form of hatred, as if we were the insti-
gators of the quarrels. They complain that no fruit has followed from
our doctrine. To be sure, I know that we have been mocked by corrupt
men for this same reason: by touching incurable diseases, we have only
inflamed them. For this is what they think: given the very perilous state
of the church, it is useless to attempt remedies, since there is no hope
for healing. For that reason, they conclude that nothing is better than
not to disturb a well-placed evil. Those who speak in this way do not
understand that the renewal of the church is a work of God that relies
no more on the hope and opinion of men than the resurrection of the
dead or any other miracle of that sort. Therefore, here the readiness to act
must be expected not from the will of men nor from the inclination of
the times, but be fit to burst forth through the midst of the despair. The
Lord wants His gospel to be preached. We comply with this mandate and
follow what He calls us to do. It does not belong to us to inquire what
success will result, but we should ask it from Him in our prayers and
desire Him as our supreme good in our supplications. We should also
exert ourselves with all devotion, zeal, and diligence, so that such may
come to pass. Meanwhile, however, we must endure whatever comes to
pass with a calm mind.

Therefore, this is unjustly attributed to us as a charge: that we did not
do as much good as we desired and others had desired. God commands
us to plant and to water. We have done so. It is He alone who gives the
increase. What if He does not will to grant our prayer? If it is agreed that
we have faithfully done our part, let our enemies no longer require anything from us—let them complain to God about less prosperous success.
However, that which they allege is also most false: that there is no fruit
of our doctrine. I leave unmentioned the correction of outward idolatry
and very many superstitions and errors, which must not be regarded as
nothing. But is this really no fruit—that many truly godly people relate
that, after they received us, they learned how to worship God with a pure
heart at last? That they began to invoke Him with a peaceful conscience?
That, freed from constant torments, they took in a true taste of Christ,
in whom they found rest? But if proofs are sought that are evident in

the sight of men, it does not go so badly with us that we are not able to boast in very many. How many people, although they were previously characterized by a more corrupt life, so repented that they appeared to have been converted into new people? How many people, although their previous lives lacked all reproach—no, rather had excellent praise—did not nevertheless so regress that they abundantly testify by their lives that our ministry is not without seed and fruit? Our enemies can disgrace us and indeed defame us with their false accusations, especially among those in power, but they will not take this away from us: among those who have embraced our doctrine, more innocence, integrity, and true holiness is found than among all those who are regarded as most distinguished to them. But if there are those who—and we confess that there are too many—abuse the gospel to loosen the reins for their wickedness, it is certainly not new. But why is it necessary for us to take the blame for that? It is known that the gospel is the sole rule for living in a good, holy way. But the fact is that not everyone allows himself to be ruled by it, and some even, having cut off its yoke as it were, more freely become proud. On this point we acknowledge that what Simeon said is true: Christ was appointed for this—to reveal the thoughts of many hearts (Luke 2:35). For that reason, if the light of the gospel shines, with the result that the secret wickedness of the ungodly is exposed, it pleases God. Hence to bring charges against ministers of the gospel and their preaching belongs to extreme arrogance and malice. But I will do no harm to them, if I hurl back at them that about which they try to inflame envy toward us. From where indeed do those who despise God obtain the audacity to run riot, except because, in the midst of the racket of the quarrels, they think that everything is permitted to them? Therefore, they acknowledge that this is their guilt: by hindering the course of truth, they foster the impunity of the wicked.

They say that we lack discipline and laws to keep the people in order. We have a twofold response at our disposal for that charge. If I should say that order has been rightly established among us, the daily sermons of our men will refute me, since they lament that discipline still lies neglected. But just as I do not deny that we are lacking in that good, so

I say that we must regard those to whom it is due (both previously and now) that we use it, so that the blame may be attributed to them. Let our enemies deny, if they can, that they invent everything in which they not only hinder our labor in shaping churches and putting them into order, but also break up and overturn whatever was begun by us. To be sure, we diligently labor for the edification of the church. While we are busy with this work, they, poised to strike, promptly hurl themselves to shake the foundations, and they do not allow us any rest, so that we may organize our own condition for the church. Later they bring the charge of dispersion, of which they are the cause, against us as an occasion of reproach. What kind of nobility is it that shows constant annoyance with us and then takes as an occasion for a charge that there is not time to organize all the parts of the church by it? Because much is still lacking for perfection, God is witness to our groans, and men to our grievances. But we have set in place several measures that pertain to discipline. That is to say, just as people usually do who undertake to rebuild a building that has collapsed, so that they pull out and gather together the scattered, heaping fragments of the ruins into a pile, to be fastened into place later, so it was necessary for us to do likewise. For if anything remained from that ancient discipline in so great a wasteland of the church, it had so lost its pristine face by having fallen down and having been mixed in that hideous heap of ruins that it could be put to no use unless it had first been pulled out of that pile.

But would that they challenge us by their own example at least. But why? Do those who complain that we have no discipline among us themselves have the same? Or would it not show that they acknowledge their vice before God together with us and confess that they put the blame on us for something that will soon be hurled back upon their own heads? There are two parts of discipline. The first applies to the clergy, and the second to the laity. I would like to know now by what strictness they keep their clergy in honest, chaste morals. I send them back to that purer and more meticulous holiness to which the ancient canons obligated the clergy. For I know that they laugh inwardly when anybody stirs up those laws—now dead for many centuries—from long oblivion.

I only ask for common decency among their clergy, so that if they do not excel in purity of life, they at least not be infamous for corruption. If anybody sneaks into the priesthood by gifts, by popularity, by corrupt allegiances, or by a secretive recommendation, the canons declare that it is simony and require that it be punished. How rarely does anyone today arrive at the priesthood in a different way? But yet that highest form of inflexibility prevails, as I have said. But how great is the shame that nothing has been required in the laws that the houses of bishops be shops for simony—open and exposed for sale? What shall I say about the papal court, where it now appears trifling to publicly make bids for priesthoods, when the bribes belong to pimps, sorcerers, and obscene criminals? If even the slightest bit of human reason prevails among us, how great is the monstrosity that twelve-year-old boys occupy the office of archbishop? When Christ was stricken with blows, was He affected by a more unworthy insult? Or can God be more openly mocked by men than when a boy is put in charge to rule the Christian people and is placed in the seat of a father and pastor? The canons decree this about presbyters and bishops: that each person stand guard at his own station, lest anybody be away from his congregation for very long. But let us think that no such thing is required.

Does someone, however, not see that the Christian name is also prostituted by the derisions of the Turks when someone is called a pastor of the church, which he has never attended in his whole life? For that someone may always dwell in that place where a pastor was appointed began to be a rare practice a long time ago. Bishops and abbots either have their own palaces or are ordinaries in the palaces of princes. Some choose a place for their own natural inclination, where they are delighted. But for those whose home is more pleasing, they truly reside in their own parishes. For they are lazy gluttons who know nothing less than their duty. That is also forbidden in the ancient canons—that two churches be assigned to one person. Let this not go unmentioned. But under what pretext will such an absurdity be excused—that five or more priesthoods are heaped on one man? That one person, sometimes even a boy, occupies three bishoprics that are separated by a great distance, so that he can barely travel around to them within a year, even if he does nothing else?

The canons require a pointed and probing examination of character and doctrine in the promotion of priests. Let us yield this to the times, lest they be bound to that excessively harsh form. But we do see how those who are unlearned and lacking any knowledge or prudence are installed without delight. Moreover, a greater account of past life is considered in hiring a mule driver than in choosing a priest. I am imagining nothing. I am exaggerating nothing. To be sure, they tell a tale, like actors on stage, that they represent a certain likeness to ancient practice. The bishops or their suffragans ask whether those whom they have appointed to ordain are worthy. There is a person who is present who answers that they are worthy. But the witness must not be sought from far away or he must be bribed. For this answer alone serves the ceremony; every private chamberlain, barber, and doorman is thoroughly taught it. Now after ordination, the least suspicion of visiting prostitutes among the clergy must be corrected according to the canons. If a person is convicted of the crime, he must be punished by abdication and excommunication. We do let go of some of that ancient harshness. But why is it that the daily visitation of prostitutes among them is tolerated in such a way as if it were permitted to them by right? The canons declare that a member of the clergy who indulges in hunting, gambling, feasting, or dancing must in no way be tolerated. But they do not in fact remove from the ministry those who are well known for such infamy. Similarly, the canons require all officers to be deposed who get involved in secular matters—who get so wrapped up in civil duties that they are removed from concern of the ministry. Let them give the excuse that this age does not tolerate such harsh remedies that cut to the quick every vice. So let it be. For I do not demand such purity from them. But who may excuse them from this— that such unbridled license to sin reigns among the clergy that they, more than any other order, poison the very corrupt world?

But the discipline of the laity works in this way: provided that the domination of the clergy remains intact and nothing is lost from tributes and plunder, nearly everything left is permitted without penalty or is carelessly overlooked. We see everywhere that the morals of men have wandered away into every sort of wickedness. But I will not summon other witnesses to this matter than you yourself, O most invincible Caesar, and you, most illustrious princes. To be sure, many reasons can be brought forth why this is the case, but this will be first among the many: that the priests, whether by leniency or apathy, have loosened the reins on the lust of the wicked. What about today? What attention do they apply to purging vices or at least to restraining them? Where are the admonitions? Where are the rebukes? What use does excommunication (the greatest force of discipline), not to mention other practices, have? They certainly do have, under the name of excommunication, a tyrannical lightning bolt that they hurl at the defiant (as they call them). But what defiance do they punish except that of those who, summoned to their tribunal for financial reasons, either did not appear at court or did not pay their creditors on account of poverty? Thus, what was a very beneficial remedy for correcting sinners, they only abuse to harass the poor and innocent. Furthermore, it is ridiculous that they sometimes scourge secret sins with anathema, so that if the secret action were admitted, no instigator may be found. To be sure, this approach is foreign to Christ's institution. Otherwise, since so many public disgraces appear before the eyes of all, excommunication ceases there. And will those, among whom everything is so scattered, still dare to charge us with disorder (ἀταξίαν)? We are, however, by no means helped by their accusation if we are implicated in the same guilt. But what I have said so far did not apply to this point—that I might clear us from that charge with which they defame us by turning it back on them—but to this one: that I might demonstrate what sort of exceptional discipline it was that they complain was undermined by us. If someone wants to make a comparison, we have no fear that at least sometimes our scattering—whatever it may be—is regarded by all godly people as more orderly than all the order in which they boast. When I say this, I am not whitewashing our faults. I know how many things could be lacking among us. And certainly if God were to call us to account today, a defense would be difficult. But when we have to respond to our enemies, we have a better reason and an easier victory than we desire.

Their shamelessness is similar when they complain that the riches of the church are stolen by us and converted for profane uses. If I should say there were no sin among us here, I would be lying. And, to be sure, such conversions of property rarely occur that do not also bring with them something inconvenient. Therefore, if there is any sin here, I do not defend it. Otherwise, under what front do our enemies direct this charge at us? They say that it is a sacrilege to convert the resources of the church for other uses. I agree. They add that this is being done by us. I respond that we by no means run off secretly, so that we do not answer for ourselves, provided that they also come prepared to plead their case in turn. Therefore, we will look at ourselves soon. Meanwhile, let us look at what they do. I say nothing about bishops except that everyone sees that they compete with princes in the splendor of their clothes, the luxuries of their tables, the abundance of their servants, the grandeur of their palaces, and finally in every kind of extravagance. But also, in their far more foul expenses, they freely spend and squander the church's riches. I remain silent about their hunting trips, their gambling, and the rest of their pleasures that absorb no small portion of their revenue. But the fact that they take from the church what they spend on prostitutes and pimps is indeed beyond shameful.

Now certainly this is absurd: not only do they take pride in pomp and glory, but they also overflow with them because they can. There was once a time when a glorious poverty was preached among priests. To be sure, it is regarded in this way in the acts of the Council of Aquileia.[26] There was also once a sanction that a bishop not have a guest room far from the congregation but have an inexpensive table and furniture.[27] But although the ancient rigor may depart, after many corruptions had already shot up together with wealth, an ancient law was also strengthened again at that time, so that there might be four portions of church revenue: one would be taken by the bishop for hospitality and the care of the poor, a second for the clergy, a third for the poor, and a fourth

---

26 Likely the Council of Aquileia in 381.
27 See *Concil. Carthag. IV. cap. 14.*

for repairing churches. Gregory testifies that this approach flourished in his time also. Moreover, although there may be no laws, as from time to time there were none (to be sure, this, as I and others have said, was born out of bad morals), nobody will not admit that what Jerome said is nevertheless most true: it is the glory of a bishop to provide resources for the poor, and it is the shame of all priests to pursue their own riches.[28] It might appear more harsh that in the same passage he also requires that the table of the priest be open to wanderers and the poor, but it is nevertheless equally true. The closer abbots come to bishops in abundance of revenue, the more similar they are to them.

Because one priesthood was not sufficient for the gluttony, pleasures, and pomp of canons and parish priests, they discovered an easy shortcut by which they could remedy this inconvenience. For nothing prevents one priest, who could swallow down far more in one month than he has for a whole year, from receiving the revenue of four or five priesthoods. There is no question of burden. For at their disposal are vicars, who readily take responsibility on their shoulders, provided that they eat a dainty portion. As a matter of fact, few are found who are content with one bishopric or one abbacy. Jerome calls sacrilegious those clerics who are fed by the public expense of the church, although they could live off their inheritance.[29] Therefore, what must be thought of those who stuff themselves with three bishoprics at the same time, that is, fifty or a hundred decent inheritances? And lest they complain that the fault of a few men is undeservedly brought against them, what must be thought of those who not only live luxuriously on the public stipends of the church but also abuse them to pay wages to pimps and prostitutes? But I am not saying anything now that is not public knowledge. Add to this the fact that, if they should be asked by what right they receive even a frugal and thrifty stipend (I am not speaking of everyone, but only of those few who reside in their priesthoods), it will occur that they will respond not even to this question. For by what services did they earn it? Just as once under

---

28 See Jerome (c. 342–420), *Ad Nepotianum.*
29 See Jerome, *C. Clericos I. quaestio 2.*

the law those who served the altar lived by the altar, so now those who preach the gospel must equally live by the gospel, and God has required this. These are the words of Paul (1 Cor. 9:9). Therefore, let them prove to us that they are ministers of the gospel, and I will grant them a stipend without reluctance. For the mouth of the ox that threshes must not be tied up. But is it not contrary to all reason that oxen that plow should go hungry and sluggish donkeys should be fed? But they will say that they serve the altar. I answer that under the law priests earned food by the ministry of the altar. As Paul testifies, the approach of the New Testament is different. And what are those obligations around the altar for which they claim that food is owed to them? Here they are: they carry out their Masses and chirp in the churches, that is, they partly play at work in vain and partly commit a sacrilege by which the wrath of God is provoked. Behold, this is why provisions are furnished for them by the public!

These are the men who accuse our princes of inexpiable sacrilege, because they have seized and carried away the inheritance of the church, consecrated to God, by force and supreme injustice, and now squander it for profane uses. Indeed, I have already testified that I do not want to defend everything that is done among us; instead, I admit that it displeases me that a better approach is not held anywhere so that the revenue of the church is spent only on those uses for which it was consecrated. All good men lament that with me. But this alone is the question of the moment: Did our princes seize and carry off the church's goods by sacrilege when they took for themselves what was plucked out of the hands of priests and monks? Did they really profane them because they applied them to something else besides fattening their bellies? For our enemies pursue their own cause, not that of Christ or the church. To be sure, I confess that grave judgment is pronounced against those who have plundered the church in order to seize for themselves what belonged to her. But at the same time, the judgment is added that, because they cheat true ministers out of their food—by killing the poor by starvation—they are guilty of blood. But how does this apply to our enemies? Well, who among their number will testify what Ambrose once testified about himself—that whatever he owned were resources for those in need? Likewise, Ambrose said that a bishop owns nothing that does not belong to the poor.[30] More specifically, is there anyone at all among them who does not equally boldly abuse what he owns, as if it were available for every expense that suits his lust? Therefore, they complain in vain that what they were holding on to without any right and were squandering by supreme wickedness was taken from them. For this seizure was not only lawful for our princes but was also necessary. For when they saw the church abandoned and deprived of true ministers, while the revenue that was said to be feeding ministers was being retained by lazy, idle men; when they saw that the inheritance of Christ and the poor was either being gorged by a few men or being carelessly squandered on expensive luxuries; should they have not lifted a hand? Furthermore, when they saw stubborn enemies of the truth jealously guard the inheritance of the church and abuse it to dishonor Christ, suppress the doctrine of godliness, and persecute ministers of it, should they not have immediately taken it out of their hands, lest they should be armed and equipped, with the church's resources at least, to harass the church? King Joash is praised by the testimony of the Holy Spirit because, when he noticed that holy offerings were wrongly being consumed by priests, he put his treasurer in charge of requiring accounts (2 Chron. 24:11). And yet those men were priests to whom God had entrusted the ordinary administration. Therefore, what must be done with those who are not carrying out a lawful ministry and not only are neglecting the restoration of the church (as the formerly mentioned men did) but are spending all their money and energy to destroy the church?

But someone may say, "What sort of administration?" Although it may not be entirely free from criticism, it is at least far better and holier than in the regions of our enemies. Hence, at least true ministers are fed, who feed the people with the doctrine of salvation. For before this, the churches, although abandoned without pastors, were nevertheless weighed down by the cost of food. Wherever there were schools or

---

30 See Ambrose, *Epistol. Lib. 5. Epist. 31 et 33.*

poorhouses, they remain. Elsewhere revenue has increased, but it has decreased nowhere. Also, in many locations poorhouses, which had not previously existed, have been established in place of monasteries. Moreover, new schools have been built elsewhere, where not only stipends have been arranged for teachers, but also boys are raised in the hope that they may serve the church later. Finally, the churches are holding in common many profits from those resources that were previously squandered by priests and monks alone. Moreover, no small amount is used for extraordinary expenses, which must, however, come into account by a very good law. It is certain that far more is consumed (while matters are so confused) than if there were agreement among the churches on a certain organized order. It would be very unjust not to allow our princes and cities expenses—such expenses that are made not for the sake of private interest but for the public necessity of the church. Moreover, our enemies are not taking away those pillages and unjust collections with which the churches were being robbed under "sacrifices," but they are lightened now. But this whole dispute is nearly superfluous for one reason: three years ago our princes testified that they would make no delay in reformation, provided that they allow themselves to be forced into the same order who are more reluctant (and that with a less noble pretext) and sin far more carelessly in administration. Therefore, your majesty, O most invincible Caesar, holds them bound to their promise. Their written judgment is also in the hands of men, so that the matter should not be a hindrance to the agreement of doctrine.

The final and chief charge that they bring against us is that of making a division from the church. And on this point they arrogantly insult us that there is no reason for which it is allowed to sever the unity of the church. But the books of our men are witnesses to how much injustice they do to us. For now, however, let them have this response in brief: neither do we disagree with the church nor are we strangers to its communion. But because by that specious title, *church*, they are accustomed to blind the eyes of even otherwise godly and wise people, I make an appeal to you, O most invincible Caesar, and to you, O most illustrious princes, first that, setting all prejudice aside, you provide an entirely new hearing for our defense, and second, lest you immediately be frightened by hearing the term *church*, that you remember that such a struggle, to be sure, existed among the prophets and Apostles with the bewitched church of their age, which you see today exists among us with the Roman pontiff and his whole cohort. When, at the command of God, they more freely inveighed against idolatry, superstitions, defilement of the temple and of holy things, the apathy and laziness of the priests, and the greed, cruelty, and lusts of everyone, what our enemies today always have in their mouth was constantly guiding them: that by departing from the common opinion of the church, they divide its unity. At that time the ordinary government of the church belonged to the priests, which they had not rashly arrogated to themselves but which God had conferred on them by His law. It would take a long time to demonstrate every instance of this. Therefore, we are content with the one example of Jeremiah. Business with the whole body of priests belonged to him. These were the weapons that they used to attack him: "Come, let us conspire against Jeremiah. For the law will not be lost by the priest, nor counsel by an elder, nor the Word by a prophet" (Jer. 18:18). There was a high priest there, and it was a capital offense not to submit to his judgment. He had the whole order, to which God Himself had entrusted the government of the Israelite church, in agreement with him. If a person violates the unity of the church who, trained in the truth of God alone, sets himself in opposition to the ordinary power, he will be a schismatic prophet who has not been so moved by such threats that he does not constantly persist to wage war with the wickedness of the priests.

We are prepared to show that the eternal truth of God, preached by the prophets and Apostles, stands on our side, and that is easy for anyone to understand. But we are pushed back by this battering ram alone: that no cause excuses separation from the church. But we thoroughly deny that that is done by us. What do they have with which they may push us back further? Absolutely nothing, except that they have the ordinary government of the church. But by how much better a law did the enemies of Jeremiah keep saying this? For at that time at least the law established by God still remained for the priesthood, so that their calling was certain. Those who are called prelates today will prove their calling by no laws—whether divine or human. Yet let them be suitable. If they did not convict the holy prophet of the guilt of schism before, let them not proceed against us under that pretentious word *church*. I have mentioned that one case for the sake of example. But all the other prophets testify that they fought the same fight when, in order to overthrow them, wicked priests abused the term *church*. What about the Apostles? Was it not necessary for them, in order to acknowledge themselves as servants of Christ, to declare war on the synagogue? And yet priests had not yet lost their rank or honor. But, they will say, both the Apostles and prophets were disagreeing in doctrine with the wicked priests in such a way that they nevertheless observed communion with them in sacrifices and prayers. I concede, provided that they were not forced into idolatry. But which of the prophets do we read ever sacrificed in Bethel? And which of the godly men do we think shared impure sacrifices when the temple was defiled by Antiochus and profane ceremonies were introduced there?[31]

The point here is that you understand that the servants of the Lord were never accustomed to entertain the empty title *church* when it was offered as an excuse to establish the kingdom of wickedness. For this reason, it is not sufficient to claim the church; instead, judgment must be applied, so that we may know what the true church is and what characterizes its unity. But this is first above all: that we may not separate the church from Christ its Head. When I say Christ, I mean united to the doctrine of His gospel, which He sealed with His own blood. Therefore, in order for our enemies to convince us that they are the true church, it is necessary for them before all to demonstrate that the pure doctrine of God exists among them. And we often say that these are the universal marks of a well-ordered church: the sound preaching of doctrine and the pure exercise of the sacraments. Indeed, this principle was established on

---

31 Antiochus IV Epiphanes (c. 215–164 BC) was king of the Seleucid Empire from 175 BC until his death. He is noted for defiling the Jewish temple in 168 BC by erecting an altar to Zeus and sacrificing a pig on the altar of incense. In response, the Jews, under the leadership of the Maccabees, revolted and cleansed the temple, an event commemorated in the festival of Hanukkah.

the doctrine of the prophets and Apostles. For Paul testifies that, if the church is not propped up by this foundation, it will necessarily collapse immediately (Eph. 2:20). I come now to our enemies. Indeed, they eloquently claim that Christ stands on their side, but we will trust them at last if they present Him in their speech. They throw around the word *church* again and again. But we ask where in the world that doctrine is which Paul made the sole foundation of the church.

Now, O Caesar, your majesty truly sees that there is a great difference between the truth of the church and our enemies arming themselves with the term in order to overthrow us. We confess as equally as they do that those who separate from the church, the common mother of all the faithful, the pillar and foundation of the truth, also abandon Christ. But we are asking for the church that bears its children for immortality with an incorruptible seed; that feeds its children with spiritual food (and that seed and that food is the Word of God); that by its ministry preserves pure and whole that truth that God entrusted to its care. That mark is by no means doubtful or deceptive which God Himself stamped on His church, so that it would hence be distinguished. Do we really appear to demand injustice? Therefore, where nothing such exists, no appearance of the church reflects any light. If the term is alleged, there is the observation of Jeremiah: wicked priests boast in deceitful words in vain when they shout, "The temple of the LORD, the temple of the LORD, the temple of the LORD," although they make a den of robbers out of the temple of the Lord (Jer. 7:4).

Similarly, we testify that the unity of the church—the sort described by Paul—is most holy to us, and we hurl anathemas at all those who have violated it in any way. Moreover, Paul regards unity from this foundation: that there is one God, one faith, one baptism; that there is one Father of all, who has called us to one hope (Eph. 4:5). Therefore, we will be one body, as well as one spirit, as he required in that passage, only if we are devoted to one God and are united among ourselves by the bond of faith. Furthermore, it must also be said again that elsewhere he says that faith exists from the Word of God (Rom. 10:17). Therefore, let this be established: holy unity will exist among us only when, agreeing on pure doctrine, we take root in one Christ. And to be sure, if it were enough to agree on any doctrine whatsoever, by what evidence would the church of God continue to be distinguished from the profane factions of the wicked? For that reason, the Apostle later adds that the ministry was established by Christ for the edification of the church, until we reach the unity of faith, that is, acknowledgment of the Son of God, so that we may no longer be children who are carried around by every wind of doctrine but, pursuing the truth in love, may grow up into Him who is the Head (Eph. 4:14). Could he more clearly confine the whole unity of the church to the holy agreement of true doctrine than when he refers us to Christ, to faith (which is contained in the acknowledgment of Him), and to obedience to the truth? But there is no need of a long demonstration of this for those who think that the church is that sheepfold which Christ alone rules—where His voice alone is heard and is discerned from the voice of strangers. And Paul confirms that elsewhere, when he prays to God for the Romans that they may think as one, but according to Christ, so that they may glorify God with one heart (Rom. 15:5).

Therefore, let our enemies draw near to Christ first and then make us guilty of schism because we dared to disagree with them on doctrine. But since I have already made it clear that Christ has been banished from their tent and the doctrine of His gospel driven out, they accuse us of this alone: we are devoted to Christ rather than to them. For whom, I ask, do they convince that those, who refuse to be led away from Christ and His truth by entrusting themselves to the authority of men, are schismatics and have abandoned the fellowship of the church? To be sure, I certainly confess that priests must be respected and that there is great danger in the contempt of ordinary authority. Therefore, if they say that ordinary authority must not be rashly resisted, we agree without difficulty. For we are not so crude to fail to see how great the disorder would be if authority were not deferred to those who are in charge. Therefore, let this respect exist for pastors, but in such a way that nothing may encroach upon the supreme rule of Christ, to whom both they and everyone else must submit. For God testifies through Malachi that He once entrusted the government of the Israelite church to the priests on this condition: that they would keep faith in the covenant that He had made with them (Mal. 2:7). That is to say, they had to preserve knowledge on their lips in order to explain the law to the people. Since the priests at that time did not at all stand by this covenant, He declared that His covenant, abolished by their faithlessness, was also useless now. They are deceived if they think that they have been placed in the government of the church with another principle than to be ministers and witnesses of the truth of God. There-fore, as long as they continue to wage war with the truth of God, against the principle and rule of their office, let them not take for themselves that authority which God has conferred (whether formerly on priests or now on bishops) only under that condition that we mentioned.

But because they are convinced that the communion of the church is confined to that kind of government that they have invented for them-selves, they think that they have won by this alone: that they charge us with estrangement from the Roman See. But a response about the pri-macy of the Roman See, in which they so greatly boast, is not difficult for us. But I will not enter that debate here, both because it would be too lengthy and because it has been addressed at length by our men. I will only request this of you, O most invincible Caesar and most illustrious princes: that you listen to Cyprian discussing by what order the true communion of the church should be regarded by you, rather than our enemies who only refer to the Roman pontiff. For when he established the source of church unity in the episcopate of Christ alone, a part of which he affirms is held completely by every episcopate, he later added the following: "There is one church, which is extended very widely into a multitude with an increase of fruitfulness. In this way there are many rays of the sun but one light; there are many branches of a tree but one oak secured on a hearty root; and very many rivers flow from one stream; although scattered plurality appears in the bounty of overflowing abun-dance, unity nevertheless remains in the origin. Remove a ray from the body of the sun, and the unity does not experience the division. Break a branch from a tree, and fruit will not be able to spring up. Cut a river off from a stream, and it quickly runs dry. In this way also the church, drenched in the light of the Lord, is extended throughout the whole world. It is nevertheless one light that is diffused everywhere, and the unity of the body is not divided."[32] For that reason, Cyprian declares that heresies and schisms arise because no recourse is had to the origin of the truth, the Head is not pursued, and the doctrine of the heavenly master is not preserved. If they demonstrate such a hierarchy to us, in which bishops are eminent in such a way that they do not refuse to submit to Christ, rely on Him as their only Head, and are focused on Him; in which they so cultivate brotherly fellowship among themselves that they are bound by no other bond than His truth; then indeed would I confess those worthy of anathema who would not acknowledge her respectfully with great obedience. But what at all does this deceitful mask of hierarchy, on which they pride themselves, have alike? The Roman pontiff alone occupies first place, in the place of Christ, and lords it over people without law and measure in a tyrannical way, no, with even more careless shamelessness than any tyrant. The rest of the body is arranged more for his standard than for Christ's. That light about which Cyprian speaks has been extinguished: it is evident that the spring has been shut off from the stream, and the very height of the tree has been cut off.

I know it is not without substance that our enemies labor in this way to assert the primacy of the Roman See, namely, in which they observe that they and everything they own consists. But it belongs to you, O most invincible Caesar and most illustrious princes, to consider carefully and be on your guard, lest they ridicule you with an empty pretense, just as they usually do to rulers. First of all, they are now also forced to confess that this primacy that they claim was established by no authority of God but the mere will of man. In any case, when we demonstrate that point, even if they do not publicly consent, in a certain manner, nevertheless, it makes them ashamed to contradict us. There certainly was a time when they boldly abused the testimonies of Scripture for the confirmation of so great a lie. But when combat was at hand, it was easy to knock out of their hands the rods that they had displayed from afar as swords. And so, deprived of the Word of God, they flee to antiquity for refuge. But we

---

32 See Cyprian (d. 258), *De simplicitate praelatorum*.

also do not turn them aside from this on any matter. For the writings of the holy fathers, the acts of the councils, and the histories make it clear that Roman pontiffs gradually rose to this height of honor, which they have occupied for about four hundred years, or rather which they partly snuck up on with cunning and evil tricks and partly rushed into by force. But so that we may concede both to them, so that they may win us over as those who concede to them that both primacy was divinely conferred on the Roman See and was confirmed by the perpetual consensus of the ancient church, there will only be place for this when and only when Rome has both a true church and a true bishop. For the honor of a seat will not stand where there is no longer a seat. In what reality, I ask, does the Roman pontiff show himself to be a bishop, so that he may be regarded as such by us? There is that well-known saying of Augustine: "The episcopate is the name of an office, not an honor." And the ancient councils describe that these are the duties of a bishop: to feed the people with the preaching of the Word, to administer the sacraments, to keep the clergy and laity in holy discipline, and lest he be distracted from these things, to withdraw himself from all the profane cares of this age. Presbyters should be assistants to the bishop in all these things. Which of these duties do the pope and cardinals pretend to perform? Therefore, let them say by what mark they want to be regarded as lawful pastors who do not engage in any part of the office, not even in appearance or even with one finger.

But, how may we grant all this—that a bishop is a person who entirely abstains from every part of his duty and that the church is that which lacks the ministry of the Word as much as the pure exercise of the sacraments—when they nevertheless oppose all of this? For several centuries now, wicked superstitions, public idolatry, and perverse doctrines have occupied the seat there, since those heads of doctrine in which the Christian religion is most powerfully contained have been overturned. Since the sacraments have been prostituted for obscene gain, Christ has been regarded with extreme derision, so that He was crucified again in a certain manner. Will it be the case that that mother of all churches, which so fails to retain not only an appearance but even a thread of the true church, will have divided all the nerves of holy communion that should exist among the faithful? At present, the Roman pontiff opposes the renaissance of the doctrine of the gospel no differently than if it were his main goal. Does he not demonstrate by that very fact that his seat will be not preserved for him otherwise than if the kingdom of Christ has been defeated? Your majesty knows, O Caesar, how great a field lies open here for me to speak. But, so that I may briefly conclude this passage, I deny that that seat is Apostolic where nothing besides dreadful apostasy is constantly seen; I deny that he is the vicar of Christ who, by furiously persecuting the gospel, shows that he is the Antichrist indeed; I deny that he is the successor of Peter who rushes at every attempt to demolish whatever Peter built; I deny that he is the head of the church who by his tyranny mangles and mutilates the church that has been cut off from Christ, its true and one Head. Let them answer me all this who so want the hierarchy of the church to be bound to the Roman See that they do not hesitate to hold the tested and proven doctrine of the gospel of secondary importance to the authority of the pope. No, rather let them not respond at all, provided that you, O most invincible Caesar and most illustrious princes, weigh whether what we demand is just or unjust.

Based on all this, it will also undoubtedly be easy to establish for you that the false accusations of our enemies should not be listened to, when they accuse us of wicked rashness and inexpiable audacity as it were, because we undertook to purge the church of the filth of doctrine and ceremonies without waiting for the Roman pontiff's nod of assent. For they deny that it was lawful for private men to do so. But what indeed was to be expected from him, to whom it was necessary to yield, so that the church could be restored to a better condition? Moreover, whoever recalls the beginnings of Luther and others who went forward will demand no justification from us. When everything was still intact, Luther humbly asked the pontiff to convince himself to heal the very severe diseases of the church. What good did it do? Since the state of affairs advanced further, even if Luther had been silent, necessity occasioned sufficiently powerful incentives to stir up the pontiff to delay no longer. The whole Christian world was openly demanding that from him. It was in his hands to satisfy the godly wishes of all. Did he do so? Now he gives impediments as an excuse. But if it is agreeable to trace the source, we will find that he alone—and nothing else—impedes himself and others. But why do I dwell on those less important arguments? Indeed, it is as if this one argument is either not sufficiently clear or not sufficiently weighty. For from the beginning until now he has shown us no other hope of coming to an agreement with him, except that, having buried Christ again, he may firmly establish (with stronger schemes than before) whatever wickedness existed when we came forward for the common good. To be sure, this is the reason that our enemies today also boldly forbid us to apply our hands to the renewal of the church: it is not that they say that it is unnecessary (for to deny that would be utterly reckless shamelessness) but that they want the salvation of the church as much as its destruction to be dependent on the will and command of the Roman pontiff alone.

Now let us look at the only remedy that those have left for us who think that it is unlawful for a finger to be moved, regardless of however many evils are oppressing the church. They are referring us to a universal council. Why? If, with stubborn minds, the greater part is rushing to its destruction, will it also therefore be necessary for us to be destroyed at the same time that the opportunity for looking after our salvation is in our power? But it is unlawful (so they say) to divide the unity of the church, which is divided when one party decides something in the doctrine of faith apart from summoning others. Then they exaggerate the inconveniences that would result from that: nothing besides dreadful destruction and twisted chaos can be expected, if each people and nation were to establish its own form of faith for itself. To be sure, this would be said rightly and appropriately on the matter, if one member of the church separated itself from the others, having disregarded unity. But that is not disputed now. Would that this could be certainly achieved: that by holy agreement all monarchs and people of the Christian world may lift a finger at the same time to demand correction of the present evils. But when we see that some shrink back from a better condition and others involved are either occupied by war or other concerns so that they are not able to devote themselves to this cause, just how long should we have put off looking after ourselves by waiting for others? Moreover, so that I may more openly reveal the source of all the evils, we see that the Roman pontiff, as much as he is able, will never tolerate all the churches to agree—not only not to hold a just deliberation, but also not to gather a council at all. He will certainly promise to do so as often as he is asked, provided that he sees all its roads blocked and every other route of access shut down. But he holds in his hand hindrances that he throws in our face again and again, so that he may never lack a pretext for being evasive. He holds all cardinals, bishops, and abbots (with the exception of a few) in agreement with him on this matter. Because they think this as one, so that they may retain the very powerful possession of the tyranny they once usurped, they are not in the least bit concerned about the well-being or demise of the church.

I have no fear, O most invincible Caesar and most illustrious princes, that what I say to you is unbelievable or even hard to be convinced of. But instead, I appeal to all of your consciences to decide whether I am telling you anything other than what you have verified by certain experience. Meanwhile, the church lingers in very great danger. Countless souls, not knowing where they should turn, are driven to misery. Also, many overtaken with death perish, if they are not miraculously saved by the Lord. Various sects spring up. Many people whose wickedness was previously hidden take out of the present disagreement a license to believe nothing. Many people who are not otherwise evil are beginning to defile their character. No discipline exists for restraining these evils. Between us—we who boast in the name of Christ alone and have the same baptism—there is no more agreement than if we professed entirely different religions. And what is most miserable of all is imminent and is now almost in sight: the dreadful division of the whole church, for which remedies will be sought in vain. Therefore, since no swiftness could be too quick to help the church amid such disaster and dangers, what else do those do, who send us off to a universal council for the convening of which no hope is apparent, than ridicule both God and men? Therefore, it is necessary for the Germans either to put off the judgment (because they prefer the church of Christ to submit to its empire) that it is perishing while they watch and remain silent, even though they could heal its diseases, or to prepare themselves immediately to take up its care. However, they will not take that second approach so quickly that they will cease to be found guilty of the offense of excessive delay. In fact, the people who introduce delay under the pretext of a general council obviously exert themselves for nothing else than to waste time with this cunning. Therefore, they must be heard no more than if they had confessed with words what they display with their deeds—personal profit is so important to them that they do not hesitate to buy it with the destruction of the church.

But, they say, such an action would provide a new example. For if any controversy concerning the dogmas of religion has arisen, it is unheard of for one province to hold a hearing and make a pronouncement. What am I hearing? Do they think that a lie, which is refuted by all of history, will convince the world merely by their nod of approval? Whenever some new heresy arose or the church was disturbed by some disagreement, were they not accustomed to call a provincial council immediately, so that they might settle what had unsettled them? Indeed, it was never the custom to make straight for a general council without first trying the former remedy. Before bishops from the whole Christian world convened at Nicaea to stop Arius, many councils had already gathered in the East. I am passing over the rest of the examples for the sake of brevity. But the writings of the ancients testify that that was ordinary which our enemies shun as extraordinary. Therefore, let that false pretext be gone.

If this superstition had seized the African bishops, it would have been too late to oppose the Donatists and Pelagians.[33] The Donatists had already drawn a large part of Africa into their faction, and no place was entirely free from their contamination. It was a controversy of very great

---

33 The Donatists were a group involved in a controversy over the validity of sacraments in the fourth to sixth centuries in North Africa. They were opposed by Augustine and eventually declined. The Pelagians, similarly opposed by Augustine, taught that man is able by nature to obey God; that is, they opposed the idea of original sin inherited from Adam.

weight concerning the unity of the church and the lawful administration of baptism. According to the new wisdom of those men, the orthodox bishops should have postponed that question to a universal council, so that they would not divide themselves from the other members of the church. Is this what they did? No, rather, because they judged that it was necessary to extinguish the present fire with haste, they stuck by and pursued the Donatists, calling them (as if to a fist fight) now to a council, now to a disputation. Let our enemies condemn Augustine of wicked separation from the church as well as other holy men of his age who agreed with him. For by imperial authority, they forced the Donatists to debate with them and, not having called a universal council, they did not hesitate to settle by a provincial council the very difficult and dangerous controversy. Pelagius also carried his head high there. A council was held immediately to suppress his audacity. When, after he had feigned repentance for a brief time, he licked up his own vomit, having stuck the spear of his wickedness in Africa, he took himself to Rome, where he was welcomed with sufficient favor. What did the godly bishops do? Did they only pretend that he was a member of the church, so that they might await a remedy from a universal council? No, rather they convened at the first opportunity and did so again and again. They condemned with anathema that wicked dogma, with which many people had already been infected, and readily pronounced and explained what must be believed about original sin and the grace of regeneration. Afterward, they did in fact send a copy of their proceedings to Rome, partly in order to break the stubbornness of the heretics more effectively and firmly with common authority and agreement, and partly in order to warn others of the danger for which everyone was to be on the lookout. The flatterers of the Roman pontiff twist this in another direction, as if they suspended judgment until Innocent, who was presiding over the Roman church at the time, validated what they had done. But this shamelessness is more than sufficiently refuted by the words of the holy fathers. Indeed, neither did they seek advice from Innocent about what they should do, nor did they defer to him to make a pronouncement, nor did they await his nod of approval and authority; instead, they tell us that they had already come to a knowledge of the cause and rendered a judgment with which they condemned the man and his doctrine, so that he may imitate their example, unless he wanted to fail in his duty to his jurisdiction. And to be sure, this was done when the churches were still in agreement among themselves on sound doctrine.

Now, therefore, when everything is bent on ruin, unless it is met swiftly, what weight do we put on the consensus of those who leave no stone unturned to block the truth of God, which they have done away with, so that it may not rise again? In Ambrose's time, there was a conflict with Auxentius about the primary head of our faith, that is, about the divinity of Christ.[34] The emperor favored the party of Auxentius. And yet he did not summon a general council under the pretense that it is unlawful for such a case to be determined elsewhere. Instead, he only demanded that, because it was a question of faith, it be debated in the church before the people.[35] And what was the purpose of the provincial councils, which used to be held twice a year as a custom, except that the bishops might consult each other about matters that had arisen, as the nineteenth canon of the Council of Chalcedon maintains? An ancient decree requires that the bishops of each province meet twice a year. The Council of Chalcedon explains that this must be done so that whatever has arisen may be corrected. But those men deny that it is lawful for the vices of doctrine and morals that have been noted by all to be addressed in any way until a universal council has come. Well, as a matter of fact, with this same pretense the Arians Palladius and Secundianus rejected the Council of Aquileia[36]—because it was not full and general. For all the Eastern bishops were absent, and few of the Western ones attended. And, of course, just a bit more than half of those from Italy had convened. The Roman bishop neither went himself nor sent anybody from his presbyters to be present in his name. Ambrose responded to all that by saying that it was not a new example that the Western bishops held

34 Auxentius (d. c. 373) was an Arian bishop of Milan.
35 See Ambrose, *Epist. 32.*
36 The Council of Aquileia (381) was held in northern Italy at the northern end of the Adriatic Sea. It condemned the Arian heresy.

a council, since it had always been the custom for the Eastern bishops to convene among themselves; the godly emperors acted wisely because they summoned the council, making the opportunity to come free to all but imposing no necessity; every person to whom it seemed right came, for nobody was forbidden. When the heretics persisted in their cunning devices, the holy fathers did not for that reason abandon their purpose. Your majesty, O Caesar, is certainly not forbidden by such examples to use this method, which offers its hand to you, to gather the body of the empire again to holy concord.

However, our enemies, who push for postponement (as I have already said), do not do this so that by differing for a while there may be deliberation for the church at last; instead, they are only looking for profit from the delay. Furthermore, they think that they will have a sufficiently long truce, if they can defer us to a universal council. But come on! Let us imagine that nothing currently stands in the way of a universal council being gathered soon; let us also imagine that it has been sincerely summoned, the day is at hand, and everything has been arranged. There the Roman pontiff will no doubt preside; or, if he is too weighed down to come, he will commission one of his cardinals to preside in his place, and he will certainly pick the one who he thinks would be most faithful to him. The rest of the cardinals will sit nearby, then the bishops and the abbots. Judges will occupy the benches on the lower level. For the most part, these people are not usually selected for another reason than that they are well-disposed to the Roman pontiff's will. It is certainly possible that a few good men are seated among them. But because of their sparsity, they will be despised, and paralyzed with fear or discouraged with no hope of success, they will remain silent. But if any should dare to speak a word, he will be overpowered by loud noise and shouts, uttered very quickly. Moreover, a great number of men will be brought together in such a way that they will tolerate anything except for the church to be restored to a better condition. I remain silent about doctrine. Would that they approach the cause teachable and in a pure manner. But it is more certain than certainty that this will be the deliberation of all: whatever is said, whatever reasons are put forth, they must not be listened to.

No, rather they will not only stop up their ears with stubbornness and determination, lest they obey the truth, but they will also arm themselves to resist with a fighting spirit. Indeed, why? Is it believable that those who allow no mention of sound doctrine in their ears, as soon as it comes to the matter at hand, will give up of their own accord? Or will we hope that those who do everything so that the collapsed kingdom of Christ may not rise again in the world will be our helpers to stir it up and push it forward? Or that those who, as much as possible, whet their swords and light fires now to rage against the truth (and others are bent on brutality), will at that time show themselves to be civil and temperate? But, so that there may be nothing else, I leave it to your prudence, O most invincible Caesar, and to yours, O most illustrious princes, to decide whether it is in the private interest of the Roman pontiff and his whole faction to restore the church to its true order and to correct its very corrupt condition by directing it to the right norm of the gospel. But how easily they are accustomed to forget their profits, so that none of them are carried by the zeal and will to take up concern for the common good by any method that they possess, you have confirmed by certain experience.

O Caesar, will you surrender the church to these men, so that they decide about its reformation by their own will, or rather by their own lust? Will you linger, relying on their nod of approval, so that, until they have agreed, you will never decree that there be deliberation for the church? If there is knowledge of such plans, they will prepare themselves an easy way out. For they will declare that everything must remain as is. But let us imagine that they are overcome, whether by shame or by your authority and that of your princes, so that they appear to display some moderation and also to release some of their power. Will they ever, for that reason, stoop of their own accord, so that having set themselves in order, the kingdom of Christ may be raised up? Therefore, to what end is the care of reforming the church entrusted to them, except so that sheep may be exposed to wolves? If it were necessary for one of two options to occur, it would still be better for the church to be regarded as abandoned and desperate than for it to fall into the hands of such physicians. To be sure, it has been appropriate for those who occupy the title and office of pastors to be the first of all people to rush to the aid of the church. It has been appropriate, I confess, for them to declare themselves leaders, but for princes to apply themselves, in such a holy endeavor, as their associates and helpers. But what if they do not do this? What if they do not want it to be done by others? What if they leave no stone unturned in order to prevent it? Must we then make sure that nobody takes action until they have lifted a finger? Must we still listen to that solemn old song of theirs—that nothing must be attempted until the pontiff has approved? Therefore, let your majesty regard this and at the same time all of you—most illustrious princes and most distinguished men—reflect with your minds on how the church, not only betrayed, abandoned, and forsaken by its pastors, but also shaken and scattered by extreme disaster, and destined for destruction, runs to your faithfulness for help. No, think of it this way instead: here an opportunity is offered to you by God in which you may display an extraordinary example that proves your reverence for Him. There is nothing that is a greater concern for all of us and that God wants us to strive for with more eager zeal than that the glory of His name remain undiminished, that His kingdom flourish, and that that pure doctrine thrive which alone should show us the way to rightly worship Him. Therefore, how much more necessary is it for princes to look after these things, to weigh them, to act on and follow through with them? That is the reason that God made them worthy of sharing His name: to be guardians and avengers of His glory on earth.

Do not, I ask, lend your ear to corrupt men, who either deceive you with the false pretext of a council, lest the church experience any relief from you; or who make light of this cause (which is the most important of them all), in order that you may be slower to take it up; or who urge violent methods of settling it. So far, O most invincible Caesar, they have wasted their efforts who have tried in any way to kindle you to rage or to clothe you with armor. To be sure, you have obtained distinguished praise for your gentleness and prudence because you have never allowed yourself to be lured away from your steadfast temperance by the trouble-making counsels with which you have been frequently and powerfully tempted. See to it again and again that this praise never be taken from you by the arrogance of our enemies. Augustine acknowledges that rule is troublesome, if heretics are deterred but not taught.[37] If heretics must be treated with this gentleness, who disturb the church out of their own wild conduct and without a just reason, so that teaching always precedes punishment, how much more necessary is it to apply civility in this case, in which we testify to God and men that we seek nothing else than that we—on both sides—may agree on the pure doctrine of God? You are the best witness, O Caesar, that the Roman pontiff together with his men lives for nothing else than blood and murder. But if you had yielded to their fury, Germany would have been soaked in its own blood long ago. And that does not lie hidden to you, most illustrious princes. Would the Spirit of God have led them headfirst into such cruelty? But that is to say this: if the lust, which has run riot for a long time without obstacle, begins to be suppressed, it will immediately give way to chaos. If there are any men (besides those) who want to see us oppressed by force and weapons, whether kindled by fans or stirred up by mindless zeal, they hate an unknown cause. For what Tertullian laments as having happened to the church when it first arose is also happening to us today: we are condemned by a preliminary hearing of our name alone, without a hearing of our actual case.[38] And what else are we contending for now, except that, once accurate knowledge of our case has been received, it may finally be judged by what is true and fair, not by a falsely assumed opinion. And it is true, O Caesar, that you have produced this very clear proof of your civility and singular wisdom: so far you have continually resisted the raging lust of our enemies to drive you to unjust brutality. But this still remains: do not indulge the destructive counsels of those who, under the pretext of delay, have long hindered and (what is worse) strive to destroy this holy work (which I call the reformation of the church).

There is perhaps one difficulty that still remains that keeps you from

---

37 See Augustine, *Ep. 48 ad Vincentium.*
38 See Tertullian (c. 160–c. 225), *In apologetico.*

beginning something: very many men, not ill-disposed otherwise, turn away from such a holy plan for no other reason than that, before they run the risk, they fall in despair of its success. But here you should consider two things: (1) the difficulty is not as great as the mind imagines, and (2) however great it is, it does not require you to be discouraged by reflection on and fear of it, if you regard it as the work of God (as we do). It is necessary that, in conducting it, our hope will arrive and our opinion will be found mistaken. It does not belong to this work to explain that first point. There will be a more fitting and appropriate place, once the time has come for serious deliberation. Let me say this only: the procedure will be quicker and less of a burden than is generally supposed, provided that there is enough courage to attempt it. But since it was announced in the ancient proverb that there is nothing excellent that is not also at the same time difficult and challenging, are we surprised that we have to struggle through many hardships for the greatest and most excellent thing of all? Next, as I have already said, unless we want to do grave insult to God, it is appropriate here for us to raise our spirits very high. For surely we measure the power of God by the capacity of our own mind, if we hope for nothing more regarding the restoration of the church than what the condition and state of current affairs promises. However weak our hope may seem, God requires us to be in good spirits, so that, having cast every fear far away, we may cheerfully undertake the work. Let us at least show Him this honor: relying on the assurance of His power, let us not refuse to find out what kind of success He wants to give us.

As the affairs of the empire now stand, it is necessary for you, O most invincible Caesar and most illustrious princes, to be kept involved in various concerns, to be distracted by the very multitude of business matters, and to be somewhat restless. But stop for this—you must certainly act first on this one matter before all the rest. I feel the energy, the eagerness, the sharp points, and the turmoil that the treatment of this topic requires. And certainly I know well enough that those people will not be absent who are surprised that I am so cold on such an extraordinary and noble occasion. But what should I do? I submit to the weight and seriousness of the matters. And so I see nothing better than to set the matter forth to you simply and without any eloquence of words, so that you may then weigh it by your own examination. Let this dreadful disaster of the church first enter your mind, which could bend even hearts of iron to pity in some sense. No, rather fix before your eyes this filthy, humiliating condition and vast dispersion that is in the sight of all. How long will you allow Christ's bride, the mother of all of you, to lie prostrate and afflicted in this way? Especially since a method for alleviating it appeals to your faith and is at hand for you? Next, take to heart how many harsher things are now imminent. Indeed, unless you intervene as quickly as possible, final destruction is not far away. To be sure, Christ will miraculously save His church above the opinion of men whenever He wills. But let me say this: if you continue to delay only a little while longer, we will have no form of the church in Germany. Look at how many indications threaten that destruction (which it is your duty to remedy) and warn that it is now imminent. They say enough, even if I remain silent.

These indications, however, should move us by their present appearance to call to mind divine vengeance. The worship of God having been corrupted by so many wrong opinions and twisted by so many wicked and filthy superstitions, His holy majesty is treated with cruel insult, His holy name is profaned, and His glory is trampled on by everything but feet. No, rather, since the whole Christian world is openly defiled by idolatry, men worship what they have devised in place of Him. A thousand kinds of superstitions reign, which are only open mockeries of Him. The excellence of Christ has nearly been blotted out of the minds of men. The assurance of salvation has been transferred from Him to the empty and frivolous trifles of ceremonies. The corruption of the sacraments must be cursed just as much. Baptism has been marred by many additions. The Holy Supper has been sold for every kind of disgrace. The whole religion has degenerated into an entirely different form. If we are negligent in applying courage to attend to these matters, God will certainly not forget it. For how would He, who says that He will not allow His honor to be diminished in any way, regard it as nothing when He is undermined and pulled down? How would He, who threatens dispersion on all people among whom prophecy has become extinct, allow the open and stubborn contempt of prophecies among us to go unpunished? How would He, who so severely avenged the Corinthians for a small defilement of His supper, pardon us, if we continue to defile it with so many heinous sacrileges? How would He, who testifies and cries out in the mouth of all the prophets that He is armed to avenge idolatry, leave untouched so many monstrosities of idolatry among us? And certainly he does not leave them. For we see that he keeps at us and follows immediately behind with an armed hand. But now the war of the Turks turns the minds of all to it and fills them with alarm. And that rightly so. There is deliberation about putting together defenses to resist them. That is also done prudently and necessarily. Everyone proclaims that there is no need for public haste. I confess that there could not be too much haste, provided that in the meantime deliberation over restoring the church to its condition, which should be first, is neither neglected nor delayed. For more than enough delays have already been introduced. The source of the Turkish war is within—enclosed in our bowels. It is necessary to remove it first, if we want to successfully ward off the war itself.

Therefore, afterward, whenever this saying is sung to you—that the matter of reforming the church must be postponed for the present moment—after other things have been accomplished, the time will be sufficiently ripe to address it. Be mindful, O most invincible Caesar and most illustrious princes, that you must deliberate about it, whether you want your empire to leave something behind for your posterity or not. But why do I speak about posterity? For now, while you are watching, what is half-ruined is sinking to its final ruin. In regard to us, however the matter turns out, this awareness will always sustain us in the sight of God: we wanted to serve His glory and benefit His church, and we were faithfully inclined toward that goal, which we finally accomplished as much as we were able. For we devoted ourselves so that all our efforts and desires had nothing else in view. We are sufficiently aware of this fact ourselves, and we have proved it with excellent testimonies. And, to be sure, since we have established that we attend to and do the work of the Lord here, we trust that He will by no means fail to support Himself and His work. But whatever the outcome may be, we will never regret that we began and advanced this far. The Holy Spirit in us is a faithful and certain witness of our doctrine. We know that what we preach is the eternal truth of God. We certainly desire, as is proper, that our ministry may bring salvation to the world. But it belongs to God—not to us—for us to attain that. If it is a win for those with whom we want to make progress, partly from stubbornness and partly from ingratitude, so that progress is despaired of and everything sinks, I will say what is worthy of a Christian man (and let whoever wants to respond to this very holy profession agree): we will die. But in death we will also be conquerors, not only because from it we will certainly pass on to a better life, but also because we know that our blood, in order to hand down the truth of God, which is rejected now, will be like a seed.

The End

A REPLY TO
CARDINAL SADOLETO
(1536)

John Calvin to Cardinal Jacopo Sadoleto:

Since you are among the great abundance of learned men that this age of ours has produced, having rightly obtained by your excellent teaching and distinguished eloquence the result that everyone who wants to appear devoted to the good arts admires you and holds you (among few) in high esteem, I am certainly hesitant to make unfavorable mention of your name publicly among learned men in this complaint that you are going to hear from me. In fact, I would not have done so, if I had not been forced into this arena by great necessity. For I am not ignorant of how great an impropriety it would be to be stirred up by any desire to harass a man who is most distinguished for good learning or that it would also be annoying to all learned men, who would think that it was motivated by no just reason, if I were provoked by rudeness alone to wield my pen against him whom they (not without reason) regard as worthy of love and honor because of his exceptional talents. But once I have explained the reason for my judgment, not only will everyone release me from blame, but there will be nobody (I hope) who will not concede to me that this cause that I am undertaking could not have been neglected by me, unless I had foolishly wanted to fail in my duty.

Not long ago, you wrote a letter to the senate and people of Geneva, in which you tempted their souls to allow themselves to be brought again under the yoke of the Roman pontiff, which they once threw off. In that letter, since it was not prepared to harshly wound those people in whose favor it was necessary for you to uphold your cause, you did what was required of a good rhetorician. Indeed, you tried to soften them with a great deal of flattery in order to allure them to your opinion. You directed whatever belonged to strife and bitterness at those whose work it was to throw off the former tyranny. And so here, if it pleases God, you rushed full speed ahead against those who with evil arts strongly urged the city, under the pretext of the gospel, to that disorder of religion and the church which you lament. But I, Sadoleto, profess that I am one of those whom you attack and slander with such hostility. For although

religion had already been established and the form of the church corrected when I was called there, nevertheless, because I not only approved
by my votes but also (as much as I was able) devoted myself to preserve
and strengthen what had been done by Farel and Viret,[1] I cannot regard
my cause as separate from theirs. But if, however, I had been attacked by
you privately, I honestly would have pardoned it with ease, out of respect
for your teaching and learning. But since I see my ministry, which I have
no doubt was established and sanctioned by the calling of God, being
indirectly attacked, it would be faithlessness, not patience, for me to
pretend not to see what is going on here and remain silent. In the church
at Geneva, I occupied the office of doctor first and of pastor second. I
argue at will that I had a lawful calling to support that province. But with
how much faithfulness and devotion I carried it out is not the reason that
I am now expressing myself in many words. I am not going to attribute
any ingenuity, erudition, wisdom, skill, or even diligence to myself. But
certainly I myself am aware and all the benefits of that undertaking bear
very clear witness for me before Christ my judge and all His angels that
I passed my time there with the sincerity that is required for the work
of the Lord. Therefore, since it has been established that this ministry
was from the Lord (just as it will certainly be clearly established once the
cause has been heard), if I should silently allow you to harshly criticize
and defame it, who would not condemn such silence as collusion? Therefore, nobody now does not see that I am bound by the great necessity of
my office and cannot avoid opposing your slanderous accusations, unless
I want (with public faithlessness) to abandon and betray the work that
the Lord entrusted to me.

But although I am presently free from responsibility for the church
at Geneva, that fact should not make it so that I do not embrace it with
fatherly love. Indeed, when God once put me in charge of it, He required
me to be loyal to it forever. Now, when I notice that gigantic snares
are stretched out for that church and danger is imminent (if nobody

---

1 William Farel (1489–1565) and Pierre Viret (1511–71) were leaders of the Swiss Reformation and associates of Calvin.

stands up to them), whose well-being the Lord willed to be my chief concern, who will advise me to remain silent and careless while awaiting its destruction? How apathetic would it be to idly and indifferently as it were overlook the destruction of that for which you must stand guard to protect and preserve its life? But a longer oration would be superfluous here, since you yourself free me from every difficulty. For if proximity (and that not very near) alone has prevailed for you, so that while you want to profess your love for the Genevans, you do not hesitate to attack me and my ministry so harshly, surely it will be conceded to me by the law of humanity so that, while I desire to look after the public good of that city (which had to be entrusted to me far elsewhere rather than by right of proximity), I am allowed to proceed against your judgments and efforts, which undoubtedly aim at its destruction. On this point, so that I may by no means see the church at Geneva as behind me (whose care I can certainly no more give up than my own soul), but so that I may be moved by no zeal for it, when my ministry (which I certainly know is from Christ and which I must defend with my own blood if necessary) is nevertheless falsely disgraced and harshly criticized, who will allow me to endure it by pretending not to see it?

Therefore, it is necessary not only for fair readers to judge but also for you, Sadoleto, to consider by how many just reasons I was forced to stoop to this dispute. Yet if it is worthy of being called a dispute, here is a simple and restrained defense of my innocence against your slanderous accusations. I say "my innocence," although I cannot do so for myself without at the same time including my colleagues with whom I shared every approach in administration in such a way that whatever has been said about them I readily take upon myself. Moreover, I will take pains to test and approve in the act itself the disposition that I have had toward you in undertaking this cause. Indeed, I will conduct myself in such a way that everybody may understand not only that I am far superior in the goodness and justice of the cause, integrity of conscience, sincerity of heart, and clarity of speech, but also that I am a little more consistent in maintaining gentleness and restraint. To be sure, there will be some things that will sting or perhaps even pierce your heart. I will devote myself, however, to ensure that no harsh word proceeds from me, except what the injustice of your accusation (by which I was attacked first) or the necessity of the matter requires. Moreover, I will also make sure that this very harshness does not give way to any excess or lack of self-control, or hurt tender souls with any appearance of brashness.

And if you were dealing with any other person, he would undoubtedly begin at no other starting point than that argument which I decided to omit entirely. For provided that he was being frank, he would point out that your intention of writing is not without a great amount of pretense; by writing, you aimed at something other than what you present as a pretext. Indeed, on any other condition than that you previously obtained great credibility for your clarity, it is suspicious that a foreign man who previously had no connection with the people of Geneva now suddenly appeals to his considerable goodwill toward them (of which no trace was formerly evident). Moreover, as a man who (practically from childhood) has been steeped in the arts of Rome, which, of course, are now being learned in the Roman court (that training school of cunning and deceitful tricks), effectively reared at the breast of Clement,[2] and now even made a cardinal, in this regard you have many marks that render you suspect to most people and to almost everybody. Moreover, that flattery of yours by which you thought that you could sneak into the souls of simple men would easily be refuted by any sentient person. But that, which might be convincing to many people, I am unwilling to attribute to you because it does not seem to me to be consistent with a man polished by all sorts of liberal learning. For that reason, I will interact with you as if you wrote the people of Geneva with the best intention, as is fitting for a man endowed with such learning, prudence, and sincerity, and as if you in good faith advised those things that seemed to you to relate to their salvation and well-being.

But whatever your intention was (for I am unwilling to charge you

---

2   Clement I (d. 99) was bishop of Rome from 88 until his death and one of the first leaders of the early church. He was author of a letter to the church at Corinth (known as 1 Clement).

with envy in this regard), I am nevertheless forced to raise a protest against you publicly (whether I want to or not) because with as many insulting words as possible you slander and strive to utterly undermine what we handed down to the people of Geneva from the Lord. For only in this way do pastors edify the church—when they not only peacefully lead teachable souls by the hand to Christ but are also equipped to ward off the tricks of those who strive to hinder the work of God. Although your letter has long digressions, its substance chiefly revolves around this: that you may bring the people of Geneva back to the authority of the Roman pontiff (which you describe as leading them back to loyalty and obedience to the church). But because their souls had to be prepared in advance for this unfavorable cause, you prefaced it with a long oration on the incomparable good of eternal life. Then, you draw nearer to the cause when you point out that there is no plague more harmful to souls than the false worship of God. You add to this that the best rule for rightly worshiping God is what is required by the church. Therefore, the salvation of those who rupture the unity of the church is at stake, unless they repent. In fact, later you contend that defection from the church is manifest, because they separated from your fellowship. Then you claim that the gospel that they received from us is nothing other than a great hodgepodge of wicked dogmas. On this basis, you therefore conclude at last with the sort of judgment of God that remains upon them, unless they comply with your warnings.

Moreover, because it greatly served your cause to abolish any trust in our words, you work on that first, so that you weigh down with crooked suspicions the eagerness for the well-being of the people of Geneva that they observed in us. And so you make the criticism that we had no other intention than to fulfill our own ambitions and greed. Therefore, since this was your tactic—to sprinkle discredit on us—in order that the minds of our readers, preoccupied with hatred of us, might not believe us at all. Before I come to other points, I will briefly respond to that reproach. I do not speak readily about myself. But since you do not allow me to be entirely silent, let me say what I can without violation of modesty. If I had wanted to consult my own devices, I would have by no means separated from your faction. But I will not boast that in it the way to obtain honors was easy for me, which I never coveted and to which, having obtained, I was never able to turn my soul. Although, to be sure, I have known several of my peers who have wormed their way into a certain place, it was possible for me to both match and surpass them. I will be content to say this one thing: what was my chief desire was not hard for me to obtain there, namely, that I would enjoy literary leisure with a decent, free environment. Therefore, I will never fear that anybody will object (unless he has entirely lost his mind) that, outside the kingdom of the pope, I sought something for my body that was not prepared for me there. But who would dare to charge Farel of that? If it had been necessary for him to live by his own industry, he had already made in scholarship such progress that would not allow him to go hungry. And he was born into a family more distinguished than one that required external aid. Concerning us, whom you pointed out with your finger, it pleased you to call out by name. But since you seem indirectly to insult everyone today who supports the same cause that we do, I want you to understand that nobody can be named by you for whom I may not answer you better than for Farel or myself. Some of our men are known to you by fame. Concerning them, I appeal to your conscience. Do you think that they were driven by hunger to depart from you, and having despaired of possessions, took refuge in that way of life as a clean slate?

But lest I make a long list, let me say this about those who were leaders of advancing this cause: there was nobody who would not be in a better place and fortune among you than who was therefore to be regarded from a new way of life. Come now, consider with me for a little while what honors and what powers we have obtained. Indeed, all who have heard us will be our witnesses that we neither desired nor obtained other resources than those which befell us. Since the people of Geneva not only had no suspicion of that ambition with which you charge us, in all our words and deeds, but also made pains with clear evidence to free us from that with their whole hearts, it is not the case as you hope that by one little word their minds can be so bewitched that they believe your empty slander rather than so much certain experience that they had with us. And we led by action rather than by words. Did we not restore to the magistrate the right of the sword and other parts of civil jurisdiction, which under the pretext of immunity those called bishops and priests unlawfully claimed for themselves, stealing it from the magistrate? Did we not detest and strive to abolish all the instruments of condemnation and ambition that they had usurped for themselves? If there was any hope of rising in power, why did we not hastily conceal it, so that they might confer it on us together with the office of governing the church? But why did we make such a great attempt to overthrow that whole kingdom or rather torture that they wrought upon souls apart from the Word of God? How did we not think that just as much was lost to us? In regard to church resources, for the most part they are still devoured by those spendthrifts. But if there was ever hope of taking them away from those men, as it certainly will be necessary at last, why did we not seek a way by which they might reach us? But when we declared with a clear voice that a bishop is a thief who converts church resources more for his own use than what is necessary for sustaining a sober and frugal life; when we testified that the church had been tested by the worst poison while pastors were burdened with so much affluence of resources that it would later cover up; when we publicly declared that we did not resolve that they would reside at their houses; when we finally gave counsel that it would be allocated as much to ministers as would be sufficient for the frugality worthy of their office and that the rest would be dispensed according to the custom of the ancient church but not so that it would overflow with luxury; when we showed that sincere men must be chosen who would preside over them, so that annually they would give an account to the church and magistrate; was this something for us to lie in wait for or rather to shake off without being asked? And certainly all this demonstrates not what we are but what we have wanted to be.

But if all that is known publicly and openly, so that no little bee can be denied, with what front do you now proceed to reproach us for the seized resources and extraordinary powers, especially among those to whom nothing is unknown? We are not at all surprised when men of your order daily spread among themselves monstrous lies about us. For there is nobody who is present either to correct or refute them. But it does not belong to the prudent man to persuade of everything contrary those who are eyewitnesses of everything that I have just mentioned, and it is a tremendous disgrace to Sadoleto by the judgment of learning, wisdom, and sincerity. But if you think that our intention must be judged by the thing itself, it will be found that we had nothing else in view than that the expansion of Christ's kingdom might be advanced by our weakness and humility. It is not at all the case that we abused His most holy name with the lust to rule. I am passing over very many other jeers that you thunder down at us with a full mouth, as they say. You call our men cunning, enemies of Christian unity and peace, innovators over old and well-established matters, seditious, deadly to souls, and publicly and privately destructive to the whole society. If you wanted to escape rebuke, either you should not have, for the sake of envy, attributed to us lofty language, or you should have restrained yourself in a certain manner from that loftiness. I do not want, however, to dwell on every matter, except that I desire that you reconsider how disgraceful it is, not to say narrow, thus to harass the innocent with many words that can instantly be refuted with one word. It is trifling, however, to treat people with insult, when it is compared with the indignity of such slander that, when you come to your cause, you inflict on Christ and His Word.

Because the people of Geneva, dissuaded by our preaching from that impure mixture of errors in which they had been immersed, joined themselves to the purer doctrine of the gospel, you say that it is defection from the truth of God. Because they set themselves free from the tyranny of the Roman pontiff in order to establish a somewhat better form of church among themselves, you say that it is separation from the church. Come now, let us examine each in order. On the preface of yours, which, preaching the excellence of eternal blessedness, occupies about a third of your letter, it is by no means useful for my response to stay fixed for long. Indeed, although the commendation of the eternal life to come is a worthy endeavor which should resound in our ears day and night, which should diligently be kept in our mind, and on which we should constantly meditate—I nevertheless do not know why you dragged out that sermon about it, except so that you might commend yourself by a show of piety. But whether, to remove every doubt about yourself, you wanted to testify that you sincerely think about the glorious life with God, or you thought that by such a long commendation of it those to whom you were writing needed to be stirred up and railed at (for I have no desire to guess what your intention was), it is nevertheless not theological that man be so addicted to himself that you do not meanwhile place beforehand this beginning for forming that life—zeal for displaying the glory of God. For we are born chiefly for God, not for ourselves. Indeed, Paul says, as all things have flowed from Him and hold together in Him, so they should be directed to Him (Rom. 11:36). Moreover, the Lord Himself, in order that He might make the glory of His name more commendable to humans, has regulated the zeal for promoting and amplifying it, so that it was perpetually united to our salvation. But since He has taught that it is necessary to exceed every concern and thought of our every good and benefit, and natural law also dictates that what belongs to man is not attributed to God unless He is put before all things, surely it is the duty of the Christian to ascend higher than to seek and procure the salvation of the soul. And so I think that nobody driven by true religion will exist by whom such a long, detailed exhortation to zeal for the heavenly life may not be regarded as tasteless, which deeply confines man to himself and does not stir him up, with even one word, to hallow God's name.

But I readily grant to you that after this hallowing our entire life should have nothing else in view than to strive for that heavenly calling. For God has prescribed this enduring rule for all our actions, words, and thoughts. And surely there is nothing else in which man surpasses beast than spiritual communion with God unto the hope of that blessed eternity. And we hardly say anything else in our sermons than so that we may stir up the souls of everybody to meditation on and zeal for it. I also firmly grant this to you: from nowhere else is there a danger more harmful to our salvation than from the devised and twisted worship of God. These indeed are the first lessons with which we instruct in godliness those disciples whom we want to acquire for Christ: they may not rashly and for the sake of their own lust invent any new worship of God for themselves, but they may know that what was approved by Him in the beginning is alone lawful. Indeed, we put forth what the holy oracle testified: obedience is better than every sort of sacrifice (1 Sam. 15:22). Finally, we by all means train them so that, content in the one rule of worshiping God that they have from His mouth, they may bid farewell to all humanly devised forms of worship.

Therefore, Sadoleto, since you published this confession voluntarily, you laid the foundation of my defense. For if you confess that it is horrible destruction to the soul when divine truth is turned into a lie by depraved opinions, it now only remains for us to ask which part at last retains that worship of God that alone is lawful. You assert this as your position: the most certain rule of worship is what is required by the church. However, we might oppose you on this point as it were, as usually happens with doubtful matters, because you call back that opinion for deliberation. But, Sadoleto, I will lift you up out of this trouble, because I see that it is useless for you to sweat. For you falsely think that we want to lead Christian people away from that way of worshiping God that the catholic church has always observed, but in the name of the church you either hallucinate or indeed knowingly and willingly make a disguise. And certainly I will soon catch you in this latter maze. Yet it is possible that you also go astray elsewhere. First of all, in its definition you omit what by all means would have helped you arrive at a right understanding. When you say that it is singular and in agreement with Christ and has always and everywhere been directed by the one Spirit of Christ in all times past as now, where is the Word of the Lord, especially that clear mark that the Lord Himself, in appointing the church, so often commends to us? Indeed, because He foresaw how dangerous it would be to claim the Spirit apart from the Word, He declared that the church must be governed by the Holy Spirit, but He bound that governance to the Word, lest a wandering, unstable entity be believed. For this reason, Christ announces that those who hear the words of God are from God, that they are His sheep who acknowledge that His is the voice of the shepherd, and that any other voice belongs to a stranger (John 10:27).

Therefore, the Spirit declares through the mouth of Paul that the church was built on the foundation of the Apostles and prophets (Eph. 2:20). Likewise, the church was set apart for the Lord by the washing of water in the Word of life (Eph. 5:26). That very thing appears even more clearly through the mouth of Peter when he teaches that people are born again to God through that incorruptible seed (1 Peter 1:23). Finally, why is the preaching of the gospel so frequently called the kingdom of God, except because it is the scepter with which the heavenly King rules His people? And you find that not only in the Apostolic writings but also, as often as the prophets prophesy about renewing or expanding the church into the whole world, they assign first place to the Word. For they say that living waters will spring forth from Jerusalem which, divided into four rivers, will flood the whole earth (Zech. 14:8). Moreover, they themselves describe what those waters of life are when they say, "The law will go out from Zion and the Word of the LORD from Jerusalem" (Isa. 2:3). Well, then, does Chrysostom[3] warn to reject all men who, under the pretext of the Spirit, lead us away from the simple doctrine of the gospel. For the Spirit was promised not to reveal new doctrine but to impress the truth of the gospel on the souls of people.

And today we directly experience how necessary that warning was. We are attacked by two sects, which seem to have a great difference between them. What indeed looks alike among the pope and the Anabaptists? And yet, so that you may see that Satan never transfigures himself with such cunning that he does not rear his head from another side, they both have the same special weapon with which they weary us. Indeed, when they arrogantly claim the Spirit, they certainly have nothing else in view than that, the Word of God having been suppressed and buried, they may make place for their own lies. And you, Sadoleto, by dashing against the starting gate, have paid the penalty of the insult that you inflicted on the Holy Spirit when you separated Him from the Word. For just as those have been stationed at the intersection who seek the road of God, so you

---

3   John Chrysostom (c. 347–407) was archbishop of Constantinople and an early Christian leader and apologist known for his eloquence (*Chrysostom* means "golden-mouthed").

will be forced to bring them in while they hesitate, having been deprived of a sure sign, whether it is more expedient to follow the authority of the church or to listen to those whom you call inventors of new dogmas. If you had known or had not desired to conceal that the Spirit shines on the church to reveal understanding of the Word and that the Word is like the Lydian stone in order that it may examine every doctrine,[4] would you have had recourse to that very perplexing and intricate question? Therefore, learn from your experience that it is no less inappropriate to claim the Spirit apart from the Word than to claim the Word itself apart from the Spirit. Now, if you intend to embrace a truer definition of the church than your own, say afterward that the fellowship belongs to all the saints, which spread through all time, dispersed through all ages, yet one doctrine of Christ and one Spirit embraced, cultivates and observes brotherly concord. We deny that we disagree on this point. Rather, as we revere it as a mother, so we desire to remain in its breast.

But here you contradict me. For you teach that whatever has been approved by the perpetual consent of the faithful from the last 1,500 years or more is overthrown and abolished by our insolence. Here I will not require of you that you deal with us truly and candidly (which should have been furnished by a philosopher, not to say a Christian), but I will only ask that you do not stoop to an uncivilized license to slander which, while we are silent, will violently hurt your reputation among pious, sincere men. You know this, Sadoleto, and if you continue to deny it, I will make it so that everyone may understand that you knew and cunningly and slyly pretended you did not: not only is there far better agreement with antiquity among us than you, but nothing else is attempted than that that old face of the church be restored at some time which was initially corrupted and defiled by unlearned men (and those not the best) and later shamefully mangled and nearly destroyed by the Roman pontiff and his faction. I will not to that degree absolutely urge you to return to that form of the church that the Apostles established, in which we nevertheless have one true model, from which if anyone turns

---

4 A Lydian stone was a flint slate used to find gold or silver.

away even the least bit, he goes astray. But so far as I indulge you, please set before your eyes that old face of the church which existed among the Greeks in the age of Chrysostom and Basil,[5] and among the Latins in the age of Cyprian, Ambrose, and Augustine, whose books create faith, and afterward contemplate the ruins that survive among you from it. Surely a distinction will appear, as much as the prophets describe for us, between the distinguished church that flourished under David and Solomon and that which, having fallen into every kind of superstition under Sedecia and Joachim,[6] had entirely destroyed the purity of divine worship. Now, will you call an enemy of antiquity a person who, out of devotion to ancient piety and godliness, not content with the present corruption of everything, strives to correct for the better and restore to its pristine luster what is corrupted and depraved in the church?

Since the most powerful welfare of the church is established and supported by three parts—doctrine, discipline, and sacraments—ceremonies are added in the fourth place, which exercise people in the duties of godliness. In order that we may show consideration for the honor of your church, from which part do you want us to consider it? The truth of the prophetic and Apostolic doctrine, on which it was necessary that the church be founded, not only has become extinct there for the most part but is banished with iron and fire in a hostile manner. Do you force upon me, for the church, what in a rage executes all the sanctions of our religion, what was revealed in the oracles of God, what was also recorded in the books of the holy fathers, and what was approved in the ancient councils? Come now, what traces of that holy and true discipline, which the ancient bishops practiced in the church, exist among you at last? Do you not hold all their institutions in derision? Have you not trampled all their canons under your feet? How, indeed, the sacraments have been wickedly profaned by you, I cannot think about without supreme horror! You have more than enough ceremonies, but when those are to

---

5 Basil of Caesarea (330–79) was bishop of Caesarea Mazaca and an influential early Christian theologian and apologist.
6 Zedekiah (reigned 597–586 BC) and Jehoiakim (reigned 609–598 BC) were two of the last kings of the southern kingdom of Judah before it was exiled in 586 BC.

have meaning, for the most part they are very inept and are destroyed by innumerable forms of superstitions, what can they accomplish in order to preserve the church? As you see, none of those matters is exaggerated by me like a prosecutor. And everything has been displayed so that it can be pointed out with the finger, if there are eyes that observe. Now, if it pleases you, test us according to this law: much indeed did he depart so that you do not render him guilty of those crimes that you have charged us with. We have attempted nothing in the sacraments except so that, restored to the original purity from which they had fallen, they also might receive their dignity. We abolished ceremonies for the most part. But we were compelled to do that, partly because in their multitude they had degenerated into a Judaism, and partly because with such superstition they had taken over the souls of the masses, so that they could not at all stand so as not to interfere very much with godliness, which they should have promoted. Yet we retained those which seemed to suffice for the arrangement of time. Moreover, we do not deny that the discipline that the ancient church had is lacking in us. But to what fairness does it belong that we are accused of having overturned discipline by those who offer it entirely to themselves alone, and although we have tried to effect restoration, they still resisted us?

But we also do not hesitate to appeal to the ancient church on doctrine. And since, for example, you have touched on certain heads in which you appeared to have a certain reason for insulting us, I will briefly show how wickedly and falsely you mock those things that were thought by us against the opinion of the church. However, before I address details, I would like to warn you to consider again and again by what account you attribute vice to our men because they zealously hovered over the explication of Scripture. For you know that they introduced such light by the Word of God in their late-night labors, so that they are thus ashamed to defraud themselves from all praise and of envy itself. It is characteristic of the same sincerity that you assert the following: the people were seduced by us by thorny, subtle questions and to that extent were led away by that philosophy about which Paul warns Christians to be cautious (Col. 2:8). What? Do you not remember what that time was like in which our men emerged? Do you not remember what sort of doctrine they were learning who were preparing themselves to teach the churches? You yourself know that it was mere sophistry, but to that extent it was intricate, confused, winding, and complicated, so that scholastic theology could rightly be called a type of arcane magic. The darker the shadows everyone was filling there, the more he was wearying himself and others with annoying riddles, the more he was returning his hand to cunning and doctrine. But when those who had been fixed in that office wanted to offer the fruit of their learning to the people, with how much skill were they edifying the church? And shall I copy all the sermons that were then in Europe and that represented that simplicity in which Paul wants Christian people to be occupied for their whole lives? No, why was it that little old ladies returned no more nonsense than they could unite to their hearth? Indeed, sermons were usually divided so that the first half was given to those foggy questions of the schools that confused the common folk, and the second half contained charming stories or pleasant speculations with which the cheerfulness of the people was stirred up. Only a few small words were sprinkled in from the Word of God, which by its majesty brought about faith amid such trifles. But when they endured our first cohort, in one moment all those tricks were shaken off among us. Your preachers, moreover, partly thus profited from their books, and partly motivated by shame and the murmurings of all, thus conformed themselves to their example so that with a full throat they might still breathe that ancient absurdity. Consequently, if anyone compares our approach of action with that and also with what today is prized among you, he will acknowledge that you have done great injury to us. But if you had attended the words of Paul a little further, any child could have easily understood that the crime that you attribute to us undoubtedly falls upon you. Indeed, in that passage Paul interprets empty philosophy as that which plunders godly souls by the inventions of men and the elements of this world, with which you destroyed the church.

Moreover, you yourself prove us innocent of your next charge, who bring forth nothing among our doctrines that you deemed must be considered, the knowledge of which is not necessary above all for the edification of the church. In the first place you touch on justification by faith, about which the first and sharpest struggle exists between us. Is that an obscure, useless question? No. Rather, once its knowledge has been taken away, the glory of Christ has been extinguished, religion abolished, the church destroyed, and the hope of salvation entirely overturned. Therefore, we say that that dogma which was supreme in religion was wickedly struck from the memory of men by you. Our books have been recorded with clear proof of this matter. Moreover, the widespread ignorance of it that remains even now in all your churches testifies that we certainly do not falsely complain. But here you will very maliciously envy us because, by referring everything to faith, we leave no place to works. Here I will not enter the just dispute, which could not be ended except in a long volume. But if you actually examine the catechism that I myself wrote up for the Genevan people when I held the office of pastor among them,[7] you would become silent, having been refuted by three words. Nevertheless, here I will briefly explain to you how we speak about that matter. First, we insist that man begin by recognition of himself (and that indeed not superficial or perfunctory), but that he may present his conscience before the tribunal of God. And when he considers the severity of that which is proclaimed against all sinners, thus bewildered and hit hard by his own misery, let him prostrate and humble himself before God. After rejecting trust in anything of his own, let him groan as if hopeless in the final destruction. Then we show him that the only door to salvation is in the mercy of God, which is offered to us in Christ, because all the parts of our salvation were fulfilled in Him. Therefore, since all mortals are lost sinners before God, we say that Christ alone is righteousness. Indeed, He did away with our transgressions with His obedience, placated the wrath of God with His sacrifice, wiped away our blemishes with His blood, bore our curse on the cross, and made satisfaction for us in death. We say, therefore, that man is reconciled to God the Father in Christ in this way, by no merit of our own or dignity of works,

---

7 Calvin wrote the first version of his catechism in 1537. Recognizing that it was too difficult for children, he revised it in 1542 and then again in 1545 and 1560.

but by free mercy. Moreover, when we embrace Christ by faith and come into His communion as it were, according to the custom of Scripture we call this the righteousness of faith.

What do you have to bite or pick at, Sadoleto? Is it not that we leave no place for works? To be sure, we do deny that even one hair avails in justifying man. For Scripture everywhere declares that all are lost and gravely accuses everyone in their conscience. The same Scripture teaches that no hope exists except in the goodness of God alone, by which our sins are forgiven and righteousness is imputed to us. It asserts that both benefits are free, so that it declares at last, "Blessed is the man without works" (Rom. 4:7). But what other notion does the term *righteousness* bring to us, if regard is not had for good works? No, if you took notice what Scripture means by the word "to justify," you would not hesitate at it. For Scripture does not relate it to the proper righteousness of man but to the mercy of God, which brings righteousness to the accepted sinner (against what he merited) and that by not imputing unrighteousness. This, I say, is our righteousness that is described by Paul: "God reconciled Himself to us in Christ" (2 Cor. 5:19). Then the manner is introduced: by not imputing trespasses. He demonstrates that we become sharers of that good only by faith when he says that the ministry of its reconciliation is contained in the gospel. But you say that the word *faith* is wide, and its meaning extends more broadly. But instead, Paul, as often as he attributed the faculty of justifying to it, simultaneously confines it to the free promise of divine benevolence but turns it far away from any regard of works. Hence there is that familiar conclusion about it: if by faith, then not by works. Again, if by works, then not by faith. But insult is done to Christ if, under the pretext of His grace, good works are repudiated. For He came to render the people acceptable to God as followers of good works. Moreover, many similar testimonies exist for that matter, by which it is proved that Christ came in order that we would be accepted by God through Him as those who do good.

This is the slander that is constantly in the mouth of our adversaries: that we remove zeal for doing good from the Christian life by the commendation of free righteousness. But this is more frivolous than greatly suppressing us. We deny that good works have any part in justifying man; we assign the reign to them in the life of the righteous. For if the person who has obtained righteousness possesses Christ but Christ is nowhere without His Spirit, it is thereby established that free righteousness necessarily has been united to regeneration. Therefore, it is pleasing to understand rightly how the individual matters—faith and works—look to Christ, who (as the Apostle teaches) was given to us for righteousness and sanctification (1 Cor. 1:30). Wherever, therefore, that righteousness of faith that we declare free is, Christ is there. Where Christ is, the Spirit of sanctification is, who regenerates the soul unto the newness of life. But on the other hand, where devotion to holiness and purity do not prevail, neither the Spirit of Christ nor Christ Himself is there. Where Christ is not, there is neither righteousness nor faith, which cannot seize Christ for righteousness without the Spirit of sanctification.

Therefore, since (according to us) Christ regenerates unto a blessed life those whom He justifies, transfers those whom He seized from the kingdom of sin into the kingdom of righteousness, transfigures them into the image of God, and to that extent shapes them for obedience to His will by His Spirit, what you deplore about our doctrine loosening the reins from the lusts of the flesh is not the case. But the testimonies that you bring forth do not mean anything else. Yet if you would like to misuse them to overthrow free justification, watch how inexperienced you are at reasoning. Elsewhere Paul says this: "Before the creation of the world we were chosen in Christ by love, so that we may be holy and blameless in the sight of God" (Eph. 1:4). Who, for that reason, has dared to conclude that election is not free or that its cause is love? Instead, the conclusion is that free election (as well as free justification) has this end—that we may live life before God pure and undefiled. For, moreover, there is that claim of Paul that we were by no means called to impurity but to holiness (1 Thess. 4:7). Meanwhile, we constantly maintain this: not only is man justified freely once, with no merit of works, but the salvation of man perpetually consists of this free righteousness. Nor is it even possible otherwise for any work to be accepted by God, unless it is approved through it.

Therefore, I receive a stunning shock when I read among you that love is the chief and most powerful cause of our salvation. Sadoleto, who would ever have expected such a word from you? Truly the blind themselves stroke the mercy of God more certainly in the darkness than those who have dared to arrogate to love the origin of their salvation. But those who have even a spark of the divine light think that their salvation consists in nothing else than that they have been adopted by God. For eternal salvation is the inheritance of the heavenly Father that was prepared for His children alone. Furthermore, who will attribute another cause of our adoption besides what is elsewhere proclaimed in Scripture? That is to say, it is not that we first loved Him, but rather that we were received by Him into His grace and lovingkindness.

That error also emerges from this blindness—you teach that sins are atoned for by acts of penance and satisfactions. Where, therefore, will that atoning sacrifice be, if it is separated from that which Scripture testifies that no atonement at all remains? Quickly mention all the oracles of God that we have. If the blood of Christ alone everywhere is set forth for the price of salvation, peacemaking, and renewal, with what confidence do you dare to transfer such honor to your own works. And it is not right of you to attribute this sacrilege to the church of God. The ancient church, I confess, had its satisfactions, but not those with which sinners might appease God and redeem themselves from punishment, but those with which they might approve the repentance that they claimed was not feigned and might strike the memory of that offense that arose from their sin. Indeed, it was not for just anyone, but only those who had fallen into some grave offense, who were commanded by the solemn rite.

In regard to the Eucharist, you rebuke us for attempting to confine the Lord of the universe Himself and the divine, spiritual power in Him (which is absolutely free and infinite) to the recesses of a bodily nature that has been limited by its own boundaries. And what at last will be the end of the slander? We have always clearly testified that not only the divine power of Christ but also the essence is extended through everything, limited by no boundaries. Do you not hesitate, nevertheless, to reproach us on the ground that we have confined Him to the recesses of a bodily nature? How so? For we do not want to fix His body to earthly elements with you. But if you had any concern for sincerity, surely you would not ignore how great a difference exists between these two things: the local presence of the body of Christ is limited to the boundaries of His body. Moreover, you should not have falsely attributed novelty to that dogma of ours, since it has always been confessed in the church. But because this dispute by its own magnitude would fill an entire book, it is more than sufficient in order for us to be spared from such trouble for you to read Augustine's letter to Dardanus,[8] where you will discover how one and the same Christ both exceeds heaven and earth in the fullness of His divinity and is not extended everywhere according to His humanity. We firmly proclaim true communion of the flesh and blood, which is offered to the faithful in the supper. We have clearly demonstrated that that flesh is truly food for life, that blood truly drink. Let not the soul be content with an imaginary conception of these things, but let it rejoice with the efficacious truth. By no means do we exclude from the supper the presence of Christ with which we are grafted to Him. But we also do not hide it, provided that local limits are absent, the glorious body of Christ is not removed for the earthly elements, and the bread is not fashioned to be transubstantiated into Christ so that it may then be worshiped as Christ. We shine light on the dignity and use of the mystery with the words with which we are able, and then we declare the usefulness it renders to us. Nearly all these things are neglected among you. For the former divine kindness that is conferred to us here, the lawful use of such a benefit having been passed over, you have enough with which it was very much fitting to dwell upon, if the people are astounded at the visible sign without any understanding of the spiritual mystery. But we have condemned that crass substantiation that you established and have taught that it is perverse and wicked—the stupid adoration that confines human minds to the elements is not able to rise to Christ—not without the consensus of the ancient church on our side, in the shadow of which

---

8 Claudius Postumus Dardanus was a fifth-century Roman politician and Christian convert who entered into a correspondence with Jerome (c. 347–420) and Augustine.

you try in vain to hide the filthiest superstitions that you belabor here.

We have refuted that law of Innocent on auricular confession,[9] which required everyone annually to recount all one's sins to one's own priest. Furthermore, by abolishing that, we followed the reason that it would take too long to recount all one's sins. But that the thing was heinous was apparent because godly consciences, set free from that dire torment, only began to rest in trust in divine grace, although previously they had been all worked up with endless anxiety. Meanwhile, I make no mention of the very many disasters that it has brought into the church that should rightly render it damnable to us. But consider this for what is done at present: it was handed down by neither the mandate of Christ nor the institution of the ancient church. We have firmly wrested all the passages of Scripture from the sophists, which they were trying to distort for it. Moreover, the church histories that are in our hands certainly do not tell us that it existed in that purer age, and the testimonies of the fathers agree with this. Therefore, it is pretentious for you to say that humility was commanded and established there by Christ and the church. For although an appearance of humility appears there, it is nevertheless far different from the lowliness commended before God in the name of humility. And so Paul teaches that this alone is true humility: what is ordered according to the rule of the Word of God (Col. 2:18).

By asserting the intercession of the saints, if you only mean by it that they with diligent prayers long for the completion of Christ's kingdom in which the salvation of all the faithful is contained, there is nobody among us who will make any objection about the matter. And so, by very eagerly applying yourself to this part, you did nothing worthwhile. But, to be sure, you did not want to lose that witty saying with which you abuse us—as if we think that souls perish together with bodies. But we leave that philosophy to your chief priests and college of cardinals, by whom it has now been very faithfully cultivated for many years and does not cease to be cultivated today. For that reason, what you introduce

---

9 The requirement of the Fourth Lateran Council of 1215 that Christians must take the Eucharist at least once per year at Easter.

belongs to them to delight pleasantly with no concern for the life to come and to hold in derision us wretched little men who labor so anxiously for Christ's kingdom. Otherwise, we have instructed ourselves on that part regarding the intercession of the saints, so it is no wonder that you omit it. Indeed, countless superstitions had to be eliminated. They rose so high that the intercession of Christ was entirely removed from the minds of men, the saints were invoked as gods, to whom the offices that are proper to God were distributed, and there was no difference between the worship of them and that ancient idolatry that all people rightly condemn.

In regard to purgatory, we know that the ancient churches sometimes made occasional mention of the dead in their prayers, but that rare and sober occurrence was contained in only a few words in which it was apparent that they intended nothing else than to bear witness in passing to their love for the dead. But the architects by whom that purgatory of yours was built had not yet been born. Those were the men who later stretched it into such importance and raised it to such a height that a very powerful portion of your kingdom is supported by it. You yourself know what a host of errors has emerged from it. You know how many tricks superstition of itself has devised, with which it deceives itself. You know how many deceits greed has invented here, so that every matter would drain men. You know how much of a detriment it became to godliness. For I pass over the fact that the true worship of God decayed very much from it. Surely this was the worst of it: while they contentiously want everyone to assist the dead without any command of God, they have entirely neglected the real duties of love, which are so greatly exacted.

I will not allow you, Sadoleto, by assigning the name *church* to such offenses, to defame us against divine law and justice, and to stir up the ignorant with hatred toward us, as if we had decided to wage war against the church. For although we confess that some seeds of superstitions were once laid down, which greatly detracted from the purity of the gospel, you nevertheless know that those monsters of wickedness with whom we wage war above all were born or rose up to that stature not so long ago. To be sure, in order to defeat, crush, and ruin your kingdom, we are armed not only with the sword of the divine Word but also with the shield of the holy fathers. Moreover, in order that I may at some time dislodge the authority of the church from you, which you often set in opposition to us as your shield of Ajax,[10] I will additionally point out in the examples set forth how far you go astray from that holy antiquity. We charge you with having overthrown the ministry, the name of which remains among you empty and without substance. In regard to the care for feeding the people, even children notice that bishops and elders are mute statutes. By plundering the land and devouring vigorous men, they prove that they are mortals of all ranks. We are indignant that a sacrifice has come into the place of the Holy Supper, by which the death of Christ was emptied of its power. We cry out against the damnable marketing of the Masses. We complain that half of the Lord's Supper was snatched away from the Christian people. We condemn the wicked adoration of images. We show that the sacraments were corrupted by many profane opinions. We teach that indulgences snuck in by shrinking from the offense of the cross of Christ. We lament that Christian freedom has been buried and oppressed by human traditions. Therefore, from these and similar plagues we have sought to purge the churches that the Lord has commended to us.

If you are able, lodge a complaint against us about the harm that we did to the catholic church when we dared to violate its holy sanctions. Yes indeed, this is now more publicly known than so that you may set forth something in denial—in all those matters the ancient church clearly stands by us, and its stands against you no less than we ourselves do. But here the thought occurs that you say somewhere for the sake of detracting from us (even though your customs are insufficiently agreed upon): there is no reason that we make a separation from the holy church. Of course, it is hardly possible that the minds of the people are not greatly alienated from your position because of the very many examples of cruelty, greed, rashness, lack of self-control, arrogance,

---

10 The Greek mythological hero Ajax was noted in Homer's *Iliad* as carrying a massive shield.

pride, lusts, and every sort of evil that are publicly evident in men of your order. But none of them forced us to try those things that we attacked out of far greater necessity. That was necessary, furthermore, because the light of divine truth had been extinguished, the Word of God buried, the excellence of Christ carried into profound oblivion, and the pastoral office overturned. Meanwhile, wickedness raged so much that nearly no dogma of religion was free from pollution, no ceremony free from error, and no little portion of divine worship free from superstition. Do those who struggle with such evils reveal war for the church, and do not instead bring help to her, afflicted with extreme evils? Moreover, you still flaunt before us your obedience and humility, because the veneration of the church sustains you, so that you do not apply your hand to exact these offenses. What obedience belongs to the Christian man with that transgressor, which by licentiously holding the Word of God in contempt commends its compliance to the vanity of men? What now looks up to and respects men with that stubborn and abrupt humility, which has disregarded the majesty of God? Let the empty titles of virtues be gone, which are summoned to cover over vices. Let us approach the matter itself without mincing words: let there be humility among us, which having arose from the least, cultivates anyone by its own degree so that it may commend supreme dignity and observance, which itself, nevertheless, is referred at last to Christ, the head of the church. Let there be obedience, which orders us to listen to the rulers and elders so that it may exact everything in compliance with the only rule of the Word of God. Finally, let there be the church, to which supreme concern belongs, to regard the Word of God with religious humility and to keep itself in obedience to it.

But, to what arrogance does it belong, you may ask, to claim that the church belongs to you alone and meanwhile to take it away from the whole world? But, Sadoleto, we do not deny that the churches over which you preside exist, but we affirm that the Roman pontiff, together with the whole flock of pseudobishops who have occupied the office of pastor there are huge wolves, in whom to this point there has been a singular zeal to destroy and scatter Christ's kingdom, until they disfigure it with devastation and ruin. And yet we are not the first to make this complaint. With how much vehemence does Bernard complain about Eugenius and all the bishops of his time?[11] But how much more tolerable was the condition of that age than the present one? Surely it is at the extreme dawn of wickedness, so that now those spurious leaders can endure neither their own vices nor remedies, on whom you think the church stands and falls, by whom we say it was savagely torn apart and mangled, and it was far removed from being destroyed in a massacre. That certainly would have happened, had not the singular goodness of God intervened.

Thus, in every place which is occupied by the tyranny of the Roman pontiff, a few scattered, torn traces barely appear, from which you acknowledge that the churches lie half-buried there. Moreover, what you hear from the mouth of Paul should not seem absurd to you: the seat for the Antichrist will be nowhere else than in the midst of God's sanctuary (2 Thess. 2:4). Should not even this one admonition awaken us, lest by chance those deceptions and tricks be aimed at us? But, you say, whatever sort of men they may be, it is nevertheless written, "Do what they say" (Matt. 23:3). Surely this is the case if they sit in the seat of Moses. But when from the seat of vanity they deceive the people with trifles, it is written: "Be aware of their leaven" (Matt. 16:6). It does not belong to us, Sadoleto, to steal from the church its right, because not only was it granted by the lovingkindness of God, but it was also severely claimed by many prohibitions. For in order to rule the church they are not sent out by Him with licentious power without law, but they are bound fast to the sure formula of the office, which it is not permitted to exceed. Thus, the church is commanded to test how faithfully they respond to their calling, whom it regards as its rulers by that law (1 Thess. 5:21; 1 John 4:1). But the testimony of Christ will not have much importance or it will be criminal, or their authority will be abolished from the least part that it

---

11 Bernard of Clairvaux (1090–1153), an influential French abbot, wrote to his former
   pupil, Pope Eugene III (reigned 1145–53), advising him on how to conduct himself in
   his office.

has adorned with such beautiful sayings. No indeed, you are deceived if you think that the Lord has imposed tyrants on His people who would be dominated for the sake of lust, when He has conferred so much power on those whom He sent to proclaim the gospel. But you persist that you do not think that they are bound by certain limits before they are invested with power. Therefore, we confess that church pastors must be heard no differently than Christ Himself, provided they discharge the office bound to them. Furthermore, we say that that very office is not to boldly force the terms that they have rashly forged by themselves, but diligently and in good faith to set forth the oracles that they have received from the mouth of God. For Christ also set down in these boundaries how much reverence He wanted to be shown to the Apostles. Moreover, Peter did not attribute or permit anything more to them than that as often as they speak among the faithful, they speak as from the mouth of the Lord (1 Peter 4:11). Of course, Paul magnificently brings out that spiritual power with which he was endowed, lest anything prevail without edification, he carry before himself any appearance of domination, or it be applied to diminish faith (2 Cor. 13:10). Now let your pontiff arrogate to himself the succession of Peter, as he wishes. Although he completely conquered it for himself, nothing nevertheless follows from it than that obedience is due to him from Christian people, as much as he has kept faith in Christ and not detracted from the purity of the gospel. For the church of the faithful does not force you into another order than the one in which the Lord willed you to stand, when he drives you to that rule in which your whole power is contained. This order was established among the faithful by the Word of the Lord—that a prophet, who occupies the office of teaching, be chosen by a consensus (1 Cor. 14:29). Whoever removes himself from it must first expunge himself from the number of prophets.

And here a very wide field lies open to me for refuting your ignorance. For you make nothing left among the controversies of religion to the mass of the faithful, unless they, upon turning their eyes away from the matter itself, give support to more learned men. But since it is agreed that every soul is subservient to Satan that relies on something else besides God alone, how wretched will those be who are steeped in such rudiments of faith? Hence, I notice, Sadoleto, that you have too abstract a theology, which is always the case for all those who have never been weighed down by any serious struggles of conscience. For otherwise you never place a Christian person in such a dangerous situation, no, in such a precipice in which he could barely hold together for a moment, since even the least would be pushed forward. Give to me not an unlearned man among the middle of the masses of men, but the most uncultured swineherd; if he is regarded to be in the flock of God, it will be necessary that he be compared to that army that was ordained by God in all the godly. The armed enemy is at hand, is imminent, and is met. The enemy, moreover, is very well trained indeed, for whom no power of the world is invincible. Will that wretch be fortified with these defenses to resist or be armed with weapons, so that he is not immediately devoured? To be sure, Paul teaches to fight with only one sword—the Word of the Lord (Eph. 6:17). Therefore, the unarmed soul is given to death to the devil when he is deprived of the Word of God. Come now, will not this be the first device of the enemy—to strike the sword from the soldier of Christ? Furthermore, what is the method of striking except to hurl doubt upon him? Does the word on which he relies belong to the Lord or to man? What will you do for this wretch here? Will you command him to seek out learned men to lean on and find rest? But the enemy does not even allow him to breathe in this subterfuge. For if he has forced him once to lean on men, he will drive and push him more and more until he falls headfirst. Therefore, he will be easily oppressed or he will regard what is right in God, leaving men behind. Thus, the state of affairs is such that it is necessary that Christian faith was not founded on human testimony, was not propped up on an ambiguous opinion, was not relying on human authority, but was written on our hearts with the finger of the living God, so that it cannot be wiped away with any tricks of falsehood. And so nothing has Christ that does not contain these elements: God is one, who illumines our eyes to see His truth, seals it on our hearts with the same Spirit, and strengthens our consciences with His sure testimony. This is that full and firm certainty (if I may say so) commended to us by Paul, which leaves no room for doubt.

Not only does this certainty not waver or hesitate among the defenses of men as to which side it clings, but even when the whole world is opposed, it does not cease to decide for itself. Hence that faculty of judging also is born, which we attribute to the church and want to be preserved intact. For however the world is shaken up and troubled by a variety of opinions, the faithful soul is nevertheless never so destitute that it does not stay the right course to salvation. Yet I do not imagine that perception of faith that nowhere goes astray in distinguishing between what is true and false and that nowhere imagines the truth. Moreover, I do not invent the obstinacy that looks down on the whole human race as if from on high, await the judgment of anybody, or show preference between unlearned and learned people. Instead, I confess that godly and truly devout souls do not always understand all the mysteries of God but are blind even in very clear matters so that (while the Lord provides, of course) they are used to submission and modesty. Again, I confess that such reverence exists among them for all goods, not to say the church, so that they do not easily allow themselves to be separated from any man in whom they have detected a right understanding of Christ. Consequently, sometimes they prefer to suspend judgment than quickly to jump to dissension. I only contend that, as long as they insist on the Word of God, those detected are never held in such a way that they are led to destruction. Moreover, the truth of the Word itself is certain and thus clear to them, so that it cannot be shaken by men or angels. Therefore, let that trivial simplicity, which you say is suited to the uncultured and unlearned, go away to look to the more learned and to change their will for the better. For apart from the fact that the term *faith* renders service to religion that rests elsewhere than in God (however determined the conviction), who (I do not know how ambiguous the opinion is) will call faith what not only is easily wrested by the devil's cunning, but also willingly wavers for the inclination of the times? Can another end of faith be hoped for with difficulty other than for it to disappear at last?

In regard to your charge that, by shaking off this tyrannical yoke, we have nothing else in view than to liberate ourselves for unbridled license, even if the thought of the life to come is given up (if God wills), judgment is carried out from a comparison of our life to yours. To be sure, we abound in many vices, and we fall short and do wrong too often. But modesty prevents me from boasting how much we excel you in every way (although truth permits it), unless by chance you would like to except Rome—that distinguished sanctuary of holiness. Having broken the bonds of true discipline and trampled upon all purity, Rome so overflowed into all sorts of offenses that scarcely ever has such an example of filth ever existed. Certainly it was necessary for us to expose our heads to so many perils and dangers, so that we may not, after its example, be bound fast to a more severe oppression. But we by no means deny that that discipline which was sanctioned in the ancient canons has a place today and must be kept carefully and in good faith. Instead, we have always testified that for no other reason did it happen that the church sank so miserably than because it was made weak by luxury and indulgence. Indeed, just like nerves, the body of the church, in order to hold together well, needs to be restrained by discipline. But how among your party is discipline cultivated or desired? Where are those ancient canons with which, as reins, bishops and presbyters were kept in their duty? How are bishops chosen among you? With what examination? With what discernment? With what care? With what caution? How are they inducted into their office? With what order? With what reverence? They only have to swear an oath for the sake of avoiding the pastoral office that they are about to meet. But it appears that they do so for no other reason than that they may be guilty of perjury, in addition to other vices. Therefore, because by entering church offices they appear to assume power that is bound by no law, they think that they can do whatever they want. Consequently, it is plausible that there is more justice and good governance, and more laws flourish, among pirates and robbers than in your whole order.

Moreover, since, after you introduced a person who would support our cause at the end of your letter, you called us guilty before the judgment seat of God, I am certainly calling you back there without hesitation. For the awareness of our doctrine stands firm in us, which does not shrink back from that heavenly Judge, from whom it certainly proceeded. But it does not dwell on those follies with which it has pleased you to play, for which there is certainly no place. Indeed, what is more inappropriate when one comes into the sight of God than to fabricate endless trifles and to assign a defense to us that is unsuitable and that will quickly fall? As often as that day enters the mind in godly souls, greater religion is produced than to free them to delight in idleness. Therefore, putting aside such delights, let us contemplate that day, the expectation of which human souls should always eagerly cherish. And let us remember that it must not be longed for by the faithful in such a way that it should not also be rightly terrifying to wicked despisers of God. Let us prick up our ears for that blast of the trumpet, which even the ashes of the dead will hear from their graves. Let us direct our hearts and minds to that Judge who by the light of His face alone will expose whatever lies hidden in darkness, reveal all the secrets of the human heart, and trample underfoot all the wicked with the mere breath of His mouth. Think now what your serious response will be for you and your people. For our cause, which is supported by the truth of God, will not be lacking a just defense. I do not speak about persons whose salvation will be placed not in legal defense but in humble confession and lowly supplication. But in regard to the cause of our ministry, there will be nobody among us who could not speak for himself in this way:

> Certainly, O Lord, I have experienced how difficult and serious it is to suffer the envy of slander among men, by whom I was oppressed on earth. But by the same confidence with which I have always approached Your tribunal, I appear before You now. For I know that that truth reigns in Your judgment which I relied upon with confidence when I first dared to approach You. Reared in its protection, I was able to carry out whatever I have accomplished in Your church. They charged me with two of the worst crimes—heresy and schism. But it was heresy to them that I dared to protest against the dogmas received among them. But

what should I have done? I heard from Your mouth that there is no other light of truth to direct our souls to the way to life than what is kindled by Your Word. I heard that whatever minds conceive by themselves about Your majesty, the worship of Your majesty, and the mysteries of Your religion is empty. I heard that it was sacrilegious audacity to introduce to the church doctrines born in human minds in place of Your Word.

But when I turned my eyes toward men, everything appeared different there. Those who were regarded leaders of faith neither understood Your Word nor cared for it much. They only drove the poor people around with wandering dogmas and deceived them with every sort of folly. Among the people themselves, the highest reverence for Your Word was to revere it from a distance as an unapproachable thing and to abstain from any examination of it. This lazy stupidity of the pastors and foolishness of the people had made it so that everything was turned to destructive errors, lies, and superstitions. They certainly called You the only God, but while transferring the glory that You have claimed for Your majesty to another they made and had as many gods as the saints they wanted to worship. Certainly Your Christ was adored as God and retained the name of Savior, but where He should have been honored, He was nearly prostrate without glory. For, deprived of His majesty, like any person among a mass of men, He lay hidden in the crowd of saints. There was nobody who truly regarded that one sacrifice which He made to You on the cross and by which He reconciled us to You. There was nobody who even dreamed about His eternal priesthood and the intercession that flows from it. There was nobody who rested in His righteousness alone. Indeed, that assurance of salvation which is commanded and established in Your Word had nearly disappeared. Instead, it was received like an oracle that it belonged to foolish arrogance and presumption (as they say) if anyone who has relied on Your lovingkindness and the righteousness of Your Son should arrive at a certain, fearless hope of salvation. Not a few profane opinions were cut from the root—principles which are foundational to that doctrine that You have handed down to us in Your Word. A sound understanding of baptism and the supper was also corrupted by very many lies.

But when everyone, not without grave slander of Your mercy, placed their confidence in good works, trying their best by good works to merit Your favor, confer righteousness on themselves, atone for sins, and satisfy You (all of which obliterate and empty the power of the cross of Christ), they nevertheless did not at all know what good works are. For, just as if they were not at all instructed by Your law for righteousness, many useless trifles were devised with which they tried to obtain Your favor. They so deluded themselves with these trifles that they nearly despised the rule of true righteousness that You commended in Your Word. To that extent, human precepts, once they began to rule over Your commands, certainly proposed to repeal Your authority, if not faith as well.

O Lord, in order that I might notice these things, You shined on me the bright light of Your Spirit. In order that I might discern how wicked and destructive they were, You displayed Your Word before my face. In order that I might rightly hate them, You pricked my soul. But in rendering an account of the doctrine, You see what my conscience testifies: it was not my intention to wander beyond those boundaries that I saw had been established by all Your servants. Therefore, I wanted to administer faithfully to the church what I had no doubt learned from Your mouth. Certainly it is clear that I powerfully endeavored that in which I labored very much. That is to say, I strove for the glory of Your goodness and righteousness to be made plain, already having discussed the clouds with which it was covered, and for the virtues and benefits of Your Christ to shine as brightly as possible, after all counterfeits had been removed. For I also thought that it was wrong for those things to lie in obscurity on which we were born to think and reflect. Moreover, I did not think that such matters, to the magnitude of which all speech would be far inferior, should be indicated in a harsh or soft way. Moreover, I also did not hesitate to detain men longer in those matters where their salvation resided. For that oracle could not deceive: "This is eternal life—that they know the true God and Jesus Christ whom You sent" (John 17:3).

But I am not guilty of any evil in that accusation they are accustomed to put before me concerning separation from the church, unless by chance I am taken for a deserter who from far away sees soldiers routed and scattered who had abandoned their ranks after they removed the sign of their leader and calls them back to their posts. For in this way, O Lord, Your people were scattered, so that they were not only not able to hear commands, but also nearly forgot their leader, army, and military oath. In order that I might draw them back from error, You offered not a foreign sign but that distinguished banner of Yours that we must follow if we want to be regarded as Your people. At this point, they threw their hands upon me who, although they should have kept others in order, had nevertheless led them away into error, and since I did not relent, they violently resisted. At this point, the conflict began to be stirred up grievously until it flared up into discord.

But now, O Lord, it belongs to You to declare to whom the fault belongs. I have always testified by words and deeds that I zealously strive for unity. But to me it was that unity of the church which began from You and ends in You. For as often as You have commended peace and agreement to us, You have showed at the same time that You alone are the bond that preserves it. If I had wanted to have peace with those who claim that they are rulers of the church and pillars of the faith, I would have had to buy it with the denial of Your truth. But I thought that anything must be endured besides stooping to that wicked agreement. For Your Christ Himself said to us, "Even if heaven and earth are confounded, Your Word, nevertheless, must endure forever" (Matt.

24:35). Moreover, I did not think that I was separating myself from Your church because I was at war with its chief leaders. For You had forewarned me by Your Son and Apostles about those who would rise to that position, with whom I should by no means confer. For the Lord prophesied, not about any people but those who would put themselves forth as pastors, that there would be ravenous wolves and false prophets, and commanded at the same time that I beware of them (Matt. 7:15). Should I have offered to lend a hand where the Lord had urged me to beware? The Apostles did not declare that the enemies of Your church would be more destructive than insiders who would lie hidden under the title of pastor (Acts 20:29; 2 Peter 2:1; 1 John 2:18). Why should I have hesitated to separate myself from those whom the Apostles announced should be regarded as enemies?

Before my eyes were the examples of Your prophets, in whom I noticed that such conflicts existed with the priests and prophets of their age. Certainly it is agreed that they were rulers of the church among the Israelite people. But Your prophets are not regarded as schismatics for this reason: when they want to restore religion that has fallen, they will not give up, even when they are opposed by violence. Therefore, the prophets remained in the true unity of the church, although they were devoured by all sorts of corrupt priests and were regarded as unworthy—they who had a place among men, not to say the saints. Therefore, confirmed by their example, I persisted in such a way that those pronouncements or threats about the desertion of the church did not frighten me from continuously and fearlessly proceeding to oppose those who under the masks of pastors scattered Your church with a supremely wicked tyranny. For I was very aware of how greatly zeal for unifying the church inflamed me, provided the bond of that unity is Your truth. The commotion that followed was not provoked by me, and there is no reason that it should be imputed to me.

You know, O Lord, and the thing itself has been witnessed

by men: I have sought after nothing else than that all controversies be dissected by Your Word and that both parties would plot together with unanimity to establish Your kingdom; and I did not decline even to dispense with my own head to restore peace to the church, if I had been arrested for making a useless disturbance. But what did our adversaries do? Did they not at once rush with violence to fires, crosses, and swords? Did they not decide that their only defense is in arms and brutality? Did they not kindle all the orders to the same fury? Did they not resist every reason for making peace? And so it happened that a matter that otherwise could have been settled in a friendly way grew into a great conflict. Although there were various human judgments in such an uproar, I am nevertheless free from every fear now that we stand before Your judgment seat, where justice, united to truth, can only pronounce in favor of innocence.

Come on now, Sadoleto—at this time good men know not that defense of our cause which you fabricate in order to burden us, but what will be revealed to all creatures on that day. But those who, taught by our preaching, pursued the same cause with us will not be lacking something to say for themselves, since the following defense will be at hand for each of them:

O Lord, as I was raised from childhood, I have always professed the Christian faith. But initially I had no other reason for that faith than what was then prevalent everywhere. Your Word, which should have shined like a lamp on Your people, was taken away from us or at least suppressed. And lest anyone should desire greater light, the notion was planted in the minds of all that the examination of that heavenly, mysterious philosophy is better left to the few, from whom oracles might be sought. The assumption is that no deeper understanding is suited to the minds of the common folk than that they subject themselves to the obedience of the church. But the rudiments in which I had been initiated were such that they did not sufficiently teach me in the lawful worship of Your divinity, direct me to the way to the certain hope of salvation, or shape me well for the duties of the Christian life. I had indeed learned to worship You alone as my God, but since the true method of worshiping entirely escaped me, I initially fell down at once at the entrance. I believed, as I was raised, that I was redeemed from the punishment of eternal death by the death of Your Son, but I imagined that redemption, the power of which certainly did not reach me. I was awaiting the day of the future resurrection, but I hated the thought of it like a most dreadful thing. And this feeling was not born in me privately at home but was conceived from that teaching that was then passed down everywhere to the people by the teachers of the Christian people. Those men certainly preached Your mercy toward men, but only for those who could present themselves as worthy of it. Moreover, they put this worthiness in the righteousness of works, so that he alone might be received into grace apart from You who reconciles himself to You by works.

Yet in the meantime they did not hide the fact that we are wretched sinners who often fall because of the weakness of the flesh. Consequently, Your mercy must be the gate of salvation shared by all, but they certainly pointed to this method for obtaining it—satisfaction must be made to You for offenses. Then satisfaction was required of us. First, after confessing all our sins to a priest, we had to seek forgiveness and absolution on our knees. Second, we had to wipe away the memory of the evils before You by doing good works. Finally, in order to fill up what was lacking, we had to add solemn sacrifices and atonement offerings. Then they showed us how terrifying Your presence must be, since You are an exacting Judge and a severe avenger of wrongdoing. For that reason, they first required us to flee to the saints, so that by their intercession You would be rendered approachable and favorably disposed toward us. But when I had performed all these things, although I had a bit of quiet, I was nevertheless still far from having certain peace of conscience. For whenever I descended into myself or lifted my mind to You, extreme terror took hold of me, which no sacrifice or satisfactions could take away. The more I considered this, the more bitterly did spikes pierce my conscience, so that no other comfort remained except to lose myself in oblivion. Yet because nothing better was offered, I continued in the course that I had begun.

In the meantime, a very different form of doctrine arose—not which led us away from Christian practice but which led us back to its source, and having cleared away the crap as it were, restored it to its purity. But offended by the newness, I offered my ears reluctantly, and (I confess) initially I firmly and fervently resisted it. For (as it is natural for people to retain teaching that they have once embraced, whether out of persistence or stubbornness) I was very slowly forced to confess that I had walked in ignorance and error my whole life. One thing in particular turned my soul away from them: reverence for the church. But whenever I opened my ears and allowed myself to be taught, I realized that the fear that it would detract from the majesty of Your church was baseless. For they taught me how different making a separation from the church is from being devoted to correcting the faults with which the church itself has been corrupted. They spoke very highly of the church and displayed great zeal for cultivating its unity. And in order that they might not appear to equivocate with the term *church*, they showed me that it is not new that antichrists preside there as pastors. They furnished several examples of this matter, by which it was evident that they had nothing else in view than the edification of the church, in which they shared a common cause with many servants of Christ whom we ourselves regarded among the number of the saints

But they spoke very freely against the Roman pontiff, who is worshiped as the vicar of Christ, the successor of Peter, and the head of the church, defending themselves in this way: such titles are empty scarecrows by which the eyes of the godly should

143

not be so blinded that they do not dare to look at the thing and examine it. The pope rose to such prominence when the world was oppressed by ignorance and dullness, as if by a deep sleep. He was certainly not appointed by the Word of God. He was ordained head of the church not by a lawful calling of the church but elected himself by his own whim. Furthermore, that tyranny with which he attacked the people of God should in no way be tolerated, if we wanted to preserve the rule of Christ among us. Moreover, very valid reasons for confirming all these points were not lacking. First, they clearly took apart whatever was appealed to at that time to establish the primacy of the pope. When they had removed every support for him, they knocked him down from his great height by the Word of God.

Then it came about, as it was publicly visible to both the learned and the unlearned, that the true order of the church had become extinct at that time, that the keys in which the discipline of the church is contained had been very corrupted, that Christian freedom had perished, and finally that the kingdom of Christ lay prostrate when this primacy arose. In addition, in order to touch my conscience, they maintained that I should not securely close my eyes to those matters, as if they did not apply to me. For it is far removed from You to allow a defense in Your presence for a willful error, since not even the person who is led astray by mere ignorance errs without punishment. They proved this from the testimony of Your Son: "If the blind leads the blind, both will fall into the ditch" (Matt. 15:14).

When my mind arose to serious attention, then indeed, as if the light had shone through, I realized in what a pigsty of errors I had been rolling around and hence was filthy with many stains and blemishes. But because it was my duty, I considered nothing more pressing than taking myself into Your way, having condemned (not without sighs and tears) my previous life of misery in which I had fallen and having been much more intensely disturbed by the recognition of eternal death, which was hanging over me. And now, O Lord, what else is left for me than to offer a prayer to You for defense, lest You justly judge that frightful defection from Your Word, from which You once delivered me by Your amazing kindness?

Now, Sadoleto, please compare that pleading with the one that you attributed to your common man. If you hesitate about which one you prefer, it is surprising. For certainly the salvation of a person whose defense turns on this hinge hangs by a thread—that he has persistently retained the religion handed down to him by his forefathers. For this reason, Jews, Turks, and Saracens[12] would escape the judgment of God. Therefore, let that empty evasion depart from that tribunal which is raised not for approving human authority but for asserting the truth of God alone, having condemned all flesh of pride and deceit. But if I wanted to fight with you over trifles, what picture could I paint, not of the pope or a cardinal or anyone from your faction who is revered as a ruler (you know very well which colors could be applied to all of them by a person who is not very intelligent), but of the most distinguished doctor among you. Certainly it would not be necessary for his condemnation to hesitate to bring conjectures against him or to fabricate false charges. For he would be more than sufficiently burdened by just, certain causes. But so that I may not appear to be imitating you by rebuking you, I am refraining from that sort of action. I will only exhort these men to look at themselves sometime and consider how faithfully they feed the Christian people, for whom there can be no other bread than the Word of God. And lest they flatter themselves too much because they now perform their play with great applause and favorable admiration for the most part, let them realize that they have not yet reached the turning point at which they will certainly not have a theater where they sell their smoke without punishment and trap naive minds with their tricks. Rather, they will stand or fall by the judgment of God alone. His judgment will not rest on popular favor but on His own inflexible justice. He will not only probe the deeds of each person but also

---

12 Arab Muslims, as opposed to Turkish Muslims.

will expose the secret sincerity or evil of the heart. I do not dare to make a pronouncement about all without exception. How few of them, however, while they lead a conflict against us, are not aware that they give the work more to men than to God.

Now, although you treat us mercilessly beyond measure throughout your letter, you nevertheless pour out the mouthful of the venom of your harshness on us at its end. Although your charges do not destroy us, which have already been partially answered, how did it nevertheless still enter your mind to charge us of greed? Do you think that such dullness existed in our men that they did not realize at the outset that they had set out to enter a way of life that was very averse to gain? Or indeed, when they charged you with greed, did they not see the great need to impose self-control and frugality on themselves, if they did not want to make themselves look ridiculous even to their own children? When they demonstrated that there is a reason for the correction so that pastors might be freed from excessive wealth, in order that they might be occupied more with care for the church, did they not willfully prevent themselves from access to wealth? Indeed, what riches still remained for them to grasp after? What? Would not this have been the easiest shortcut to wealth and honors—to do business with you from the beginning by those agreements that were offered? How much would your pontiff have paid for their silence at that time? How much would he pay for the same today? Why, if they are motivated in the least by lust for possessions, did they give up every hope of increasing their possessions, thus preferring to be poor constantly than to get rich instantly without much difficulty? But ambition restrains them, of course. I do not understand the reason that you have for this charge. For those who first began this cause could expect nothing else than to be despised by the whole world. Moreover, those who later joined the cause knowingly and willingly exposed themselves to the endless slander and criticism of the whole world. But where is deceit and inner malice in them? Certainly no suspicion of those things clings to us. Therefore, discuss them in your holy college, where they are constantly at work.

Because I am hastening to the end, I am forced to omit your slander that, relying on our own wisdom, we find nobody in the whole church whom we deem worthy of any trust. But I have already sufficiently demonstrated that it is slander. For although we have established that the Word of God alone exists beyond every possible judgment, we nevertheless wanted to grant certain authority to councils and the fathers, provided that they correspond to its norm. Moreover, we grant councils and the fathers that honor and place that is appropriate to obtain under Christ. But the most serious charge of all is that we tried to split the bride of Christ. If that were true, you and the whole world would rightly regard us as hopeless. But I will take that charge against us no differently if you do not contend that the bride of Christ is split by those who want to present her to Christ as a pure virgin, are stirred up with holy zeal to keep her unblemished in Christ, call her back to conjugal fidelity after she was corrupted by wicked seductions, and do not hesitate to make war against all adulterers who set traps for her purity. And what else did we do? Had not the purity of the church been tempted and indeed violated by wandering doctrines from your faction? Had it not been violently prostituted by you with your endless superstitions? Had it not been defiled by the filthiest kind of adultery—the worship of images? That is to say, because we did not let you hold the most holy chamber of Christ in such contempt, we are said to have severed His bride. But I say that the severing of which you accuse us is obviously conspicuous among you. Moreover, that is not the case only in the church but also in Christ Himself, who has indeed been wretchedly dissected. How does the church cling to her husband whom she does not securely have? Moreover, where is the presence of Christ when the glory of His righteousness, holiness, and wisdom is transferred elsewhere?

But before we stirred up the conflict, everything was very calm and at peace. Certainly among pastors and laypersons idleness and laziness took effect so that there were almost no controversies over religion. How intensely, however, did the sophists debate in the schools! It is not right, therefore, for you to attribute a peaceful kingdom to your people, where there was quiet only because Christ kept silent. I admit that after the new rise of the gospel, great conflicts raged, before which there was quiet.

But that is unjustly imputed to our men, who sought nothing else in their course of action than, having restored religion, to gather together the churches that were scattered and dispersed by discord in true unity. And lest I repeat the same material, why did they refuse to accept such, in order to restore peace to the churches? But while you strive against us, every attempt is made in vain. But because they desire to have peace, with which you can overturn in one day what they took many months to build for the glory of Christ.

I will not overwhelm you with many words, because one word can make the matter clear. Our men offered to render an account of their doctrine. If your men were defeated in an argument, they refused to concede. Who now is responsible that the church does not enjoy perfect peace and the light of truth? Go ahead and call those of us seditious who do not allow the church to be at peace! But lest you omit anything that could do no harm to our cause, because many sects have arisen in the last few years and you are jealous, you turn them against us for the sake of your fairness. For if we are therefore worthy of hatred, the Christian name in former times also produced just hatred among the wicked. So, stop harassing us on this point, or publicly declare that the Christian religion must be removed from human memory, which produces so much commotion in the world! Therefore, it should by no means stand in the way of our cause that Satan has tried in every way to hinder the work of Christ. This question is more relevant—who has been diligent to ward off all the sects that have sprung up? But certainly we alone, while you were idle and snoring, undertook this entire effort. May the Lord grant, Sadoleto, you and all the rest of your people to understand sometime that there is no other bond of unity than if Christ the Lord, who has reconciled us to God the Father, gathers us from the separation into the fellowship of His body, so that we may join together in one heart and mind by His one Word and Spirit.

Strasbourg, September 1, 1539

SUBJECT INDEX

Dr. Casey Carmichael is an independent scholar in Belleville, Ill. He earned an M.A. in classics at the University of Kentucky and a doctorate in theology at the University of Geneva. Dr. Carmichael has published two translations with Reformation Heritage Books and has two forthcoming translations in *Reformation and Renaissance Review*.

Dr. W. Robert Godfrey is a Ligonier Ministries teaching fellow and chairman of Ligonier Ministries. He is president emeritus and professor emeritus of church history at Westminster Seminary California and an ordained minister in the United Reformed Churches in North America. He is a graduate of Stanford University (A.B., M.A., and Ph.D.) and Gordon-Conwell Theological Seminary (M.Div.).

He is the featured teacher for the six-part Ligonier teaching series *A Survey of Church History*. He is author of several books, including *John Calvin: Pilgrim and Pastor* and *Saving the Reformation: The Pastoral Theology of the Canons of Dort*.